W9-DAC-999

Altering
Men's
Ready-to-Wear

Mary A. Roehr

Copyright 1987 Mary A. Roehr

Revised for Reprint 1991

All rights reserved. No part of this book may be reproduced in any form or by any process without permission in writing from the copyright owner.

ISBN 0-9619229-1-5

Printed in U.S.A

Dedicated to my brother,

Michael Peter Kalosh,

who has exquisite taste in clothing.

Table of Contents

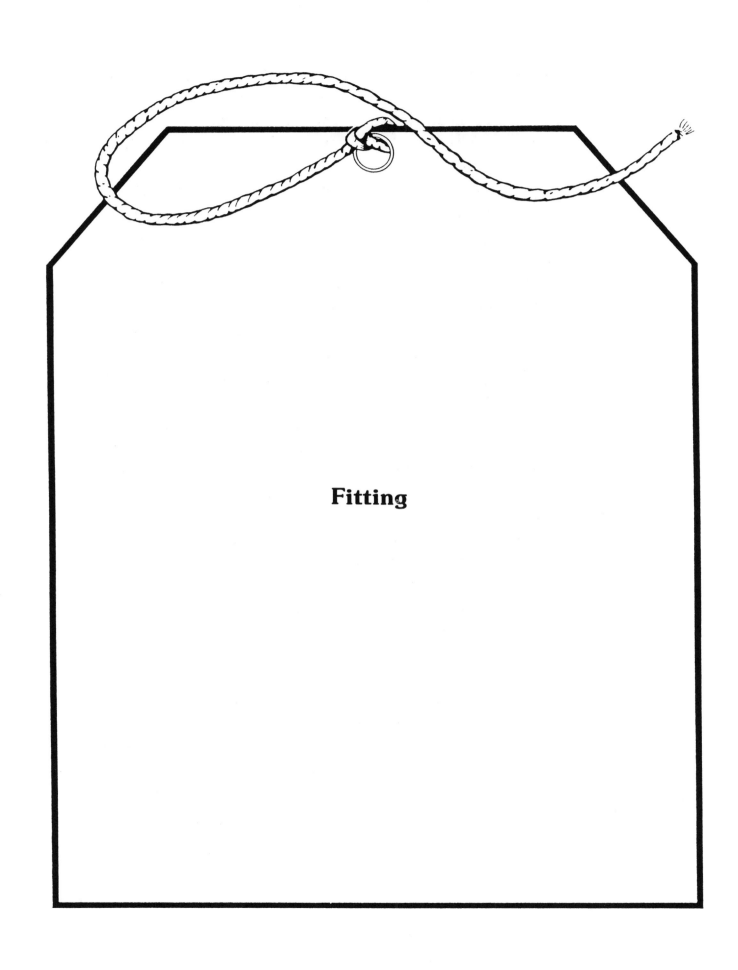

Fitting

If you have not done alterations on men's clothing before, you will be surprised at how much easier men are to fit than women. This is because men have fewer curves in less places, resulting in more standardized alterations.

When a women's garment doesn't fit, there could be several different ways to alter it. When a man's garment doesn't fit, there is usually one set way to fix the problem and it will work consistently.

Laying the groundwork for a successful fitting will begin before you even see the customer. First of all, arrange your fitting area so it will be of optimum use to you and of optimum comfort to your customer. You must have either a separate dressing room or an area that can be closed off for privacy. Have hooks and hangers for clothing and a chair or seat. Make the space large enough so the customer will not be uncomfortable or inconvenienced while he is changing. Men need more room than women, as well as sturdier surroundings.

In general, men dislike trying on clothing, so fit them as quickly and efficiently as possible.

It is very important to have proper lighting and a full-length mirror. A three-way mirror is ideal. If you only have room for one, make it at least six feet in length, taking into consideration the average height of men.

Measuring tape, pins, and marking chalk within arm's length of your mirror will enable you to fit without stepping away. Don't forget clips, clothespins, or whatever marking devices you use for ultrasuede or leathers which cannot be marked the conventional ways. Pen, paper, order pad, lint brush, and business cards should also be in this immediate area.

Your first contact with a customer may be on the telephone. Always answer in a businesslike way, such as, "Good morning. This is Always Alterations. How can I help you?" If you are working in a shop, this will become matter of course. If you are working in your home and choose not to install a separate business line, it is very important to have family members understand the necessity of good phone manners. Children in particular will need to be educated to take and receive messages accurately. Help them by practicing what you would like them to say and have a pencil and paper readily available at all extensions.

In general, men look at clothing and alterations as investments and they will seldom inquire about price. If they do ask for a price on the phone, gather as many details as possible in order to get a precise picture of what he expects. Because men's alterations are more standardized than women's, you should be able to give a fairly accurate price estimate on the phone, but make sure the customer knows it is just that. After examining the garment firsthand, you can give a definite price quote.

If you are going to see customers by appointment only, say so from the beginning. You will be communicating the fact that you have other customers, but each will receive your exclusive attention at his allotted time. Tell the customer what he needs to bring to the first appointment, such as the shoes he will be wearing with the garment. Give specific directions to your place of business and mention any special parking or entrance accommodations. Get the customer's telephone number and repeat the appointment time and date.

During the initial fitting with the customer, never underestimate the power of a first impression. Even without speaking, many facts can be communicated such as approximate age, nationality, occupation, interests, religion, economic status, and marital status. By simple body language we convey personality characteristics like patience, assertiveness, shyness, friendliness, cautiousness, and confidence. By observing people's actions, we can tell if they are willing to participate, if they are distracted, or if they are embarrassed.

Because of this, try to make the most of the first impression your customer receives from you. Since you are working in the clothing profession, the way you dress will be of primary importance. This does not mean you have to own an extensive high-fashion wardrobe, but your ability to sew and fit should be evident on you. Your clothing should be clean, becoming, and comfortable. A few well-fitting classic styles will go a lot farther than a closet full of trendy impulse items. If you are a woman, strictly avoid low cut, clingy, or short styles which draw attention to your figure. Go out of your way to look professional, not sexey.

Convey a courteous but businesslike manner with your speech and gestures. Put yourself in the customer's position and do everything you can to put him at ease. Greet him pleasantly using his name if you know it, and introduce yourself. Show him where to stand, sit, change clothes, put his coat, and wait.

During the fitting, you will need to constantly question and instruct the customer. Position him in front of the mirror and ask him to stand on both feet.

This is necessary because the hem of the garment as well as the general set of the garment will change if he looks down or twists.

For a customer who appears nervous or embarrassed, you can "break the ice" by firmly touching his shoulder while positioning him in front of the mirror. Stand behind and to one side of the customer and view the garment in the mirror just as he sees it. Explain what you are doing as you go by saying, "I will pin the sides," "I'll mark the hem," or, "Stand still and I will go around you."

Men usually consider their clothing as utilitarian, while women are concerned with fashion and body image. Men have fewer styles of clothing to choose from also, and options for different alterations will be fewer.

When the customer emerges from the dressing room, and it is not immediately apparent what needs to be altered, simply ask, "And how can I help you today?" Wait for his response and proceed accordingly.

You will greatly enhance customer relations by reserving your professional, and personal, opinion until asked for it. Remember, some people prefer clothing tighter or looser than the norm; or, they actually want to wear their pants at a length you would consider "high waters." Try not to counsel the customer unless you foresee a problem that could arise from his instructions. For example, "I will be glad to take the pants in this much, but I must caution you that it will cause the pockets to gap open," or, "Taking the sides in this much will cause the pockets to gap slightly. Will this be a problem for you?"

If a fitting problem is extremely obvious to you but not to the customer, try to mention it very tactfully. For instance, "I think if the sleeves were shortened they would be in better proportion." Of course, if the customer asks you to recommend what can be done to improve the fit, give your advice as politely and as honestly as possible.

A general rule is to fit from the top down. On a shirt, vest, or coat, check and pin the collar area first. Then proceed to the shoulders, sides, and last of all to the length of sleeves or hem. With pants, go from the waist to the sides, and finish with the hem. Any alteration done within the body of the garment will affect the length so it must be pinned first. Sometimes you will find it necessary to sew the alteration in the body of the garment and have the customer return for a fitting on length.

While fitting, ask the customer his preference. Say, "How does that look?", "Do you like it tighter?", or "Shall I make it shorter?" Use socially acceptable terms when referring to parts of the body, such as hips instead of "buns." Refer to an extra roll of fat as extra width or say, "You are fuller here." Replace skinny with slender or thin.

Don't try to avoid a handicap or deformity, for that may be the reason the customer needs your help. On the other hand, try not to be shocked or to stare. Treat it as a part of the whole. Address the problem and go about solving it.

You will come into contact with varied conditions that will make it impossible to complete certain alterations. Try to anticipate these by examining the garment before the customer leaves. Usually the garment cannot be altered if the customer has lost more than thirty-five pounds. If the garment is cut off-grain there is nothing that can be done to correct it unless the error is very slight. Quite often hems cannot be lengthened because of lack of fabric or because the old hemline shows. Sometimes a facing will help or topstitching over the old line will do the trick, but make sure the customer agrees in advance to your method.

Inability to match thread, zippers, or other findings is a dilemma and can inspire creativity. If reweaving is an impossibility, unusual rips and tears will have to be mended as best you can, remembering to inform the customer of the situation.

If your machine simply won't handle leather or other special fabrics, don't take the chance of ruining a garment by trying to force it. Along the same lines, if you come across an alteration that is beyond your skill level at the time, simply state that you do not do that type of alteration. Don't destroy future business by trying and failing, and don't destroy the customer's confidence in you by saying you don't know how. Practice on an old or discarded garment and next time you will be able to accept the job.

It is very unhealthy and unpleasant to work on a soiled garment. In fact, some states have laws that garments must be cleaned before they can be altered. An easy way to avoid embarrassing confrontations with customers is to have a simple sign in the dressing room which states, "Please have garments cleaned prior to altering. Thank you!", or, "Thank you for having your garment cleaned prior to altering!"

Before the customer leaves, record as many details as possible on the receipt pad. Get his name, address, and phone number. Describe the garment in writing and record what work is to be done. Record special details like "topstitched" or "hand stitched hem." Date the receipt and state your terms for payment so they are understood from the beginning. You will find that men quite often expect to make a down payment. If you collect one, record it and calculate the balance.

Examine the garment for stains or tears and politely call them to the customer's attention so you will not be held responsible for them later. When the fitting is over, hang the garment neatly rather than leaving it on the floor or over a chair. Give the customer a time estimate for completion or set up the next appointment.

SAMPLE RECEIPT PAD

			101	
PHONE			DATE	
	776-4532		10/21	
CUSTOMER'S NAME				
	Nofflet Sivenson			
ADDRESS				
	1021 Crestview Dr.			
	City 93742			
QUAN.	DESCRIPTION		PRICE	AMT.
1	Grey Pant - shorten		6	00
1	Grey Coat - shorten sleeves (vents)		9	50
1	Grey vest - sides in		7	50
			23	00
	less down		10	00
	due on delivery		13	00

8

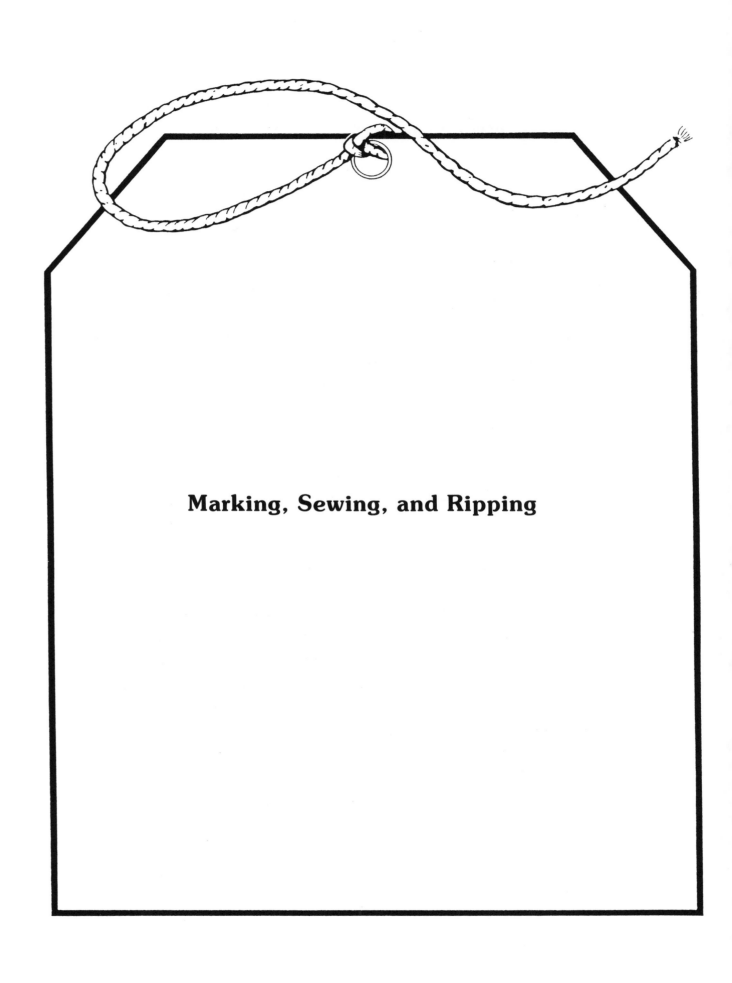

Marking, Sewing, and Ripping

Later in this book, each specific alteration will be outlined in detail, but first I would like to discuss some general guidelines for marking, sewing, and ripping.

Although chalk is traditionally used for marking men's alterations, there will be times when pins are needed.

Plastic or glass headed pins are by far the most convenient to use and have the added benefit of being easy to see both in the garment and in the carpeting. Buy only rustproof pins which will be brass, nickel-plated steel, or stainless steel. Virtually all pins are stainless steel today, but check the composition of "bargain bin" pins that seem to be a good buy. You will quickly lose the money you saved by ruining one customer's garment with rust spots. If you have never used one, you may want to try using a wrist pin cushion for easy accessibility during fitting.

As you become more experienced in marking, I believe you will come to appreciate the advantages of using tailor's chalk. It will allow you to mark much faster than you can with pins and you will not lose the mark as a result of the pin falling out. Pins are necessary for pinning out excess fabric, but chalk can be used in almost every other situation.

Tailor's chalk comes in thin rectangular cakes of two kinds, the first being composed of a waxlike substance. It is perfect for marking wool, dark fabrics, and some washables like cotton. This type of chalk can be sharpened to a fine point with a razor blade and will enable you to make clear and precise marks. The marks will vanish with the touch of an iron.

The other type of chalk is just like real chalk but firmer. It is better for silks, linings, or delicate fabrics because it can be brushed off. The wax chalk will leave a greasy mark when used on these fabrics. Regular chalkboard chalk can be substituted, but it does not have a narrow edge and your marks can become very inaccurate.

Both types of chalk come in a variety of colors but I find plain white is the most reliable and stain proof. They can be found in pencil form or with special holders.

There are distinctive marks made with chalk which form a universal language among tailors and alterationists. A simple straight broken line means either "take in" or "shorten." A broken line with slash marks means "let out" or "lengthen." When taking garments in (making them smaller), pins are usually used so the customer can see how the garment will fit.

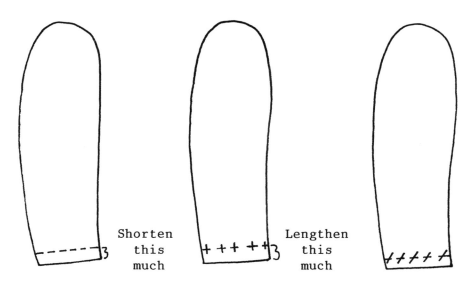

Straight broken line means "shorten" the sleeve.

Broken line with perpendicular slashes means "lengthen this much."

Broken line with diagonal slashes means "lengthen all possible."

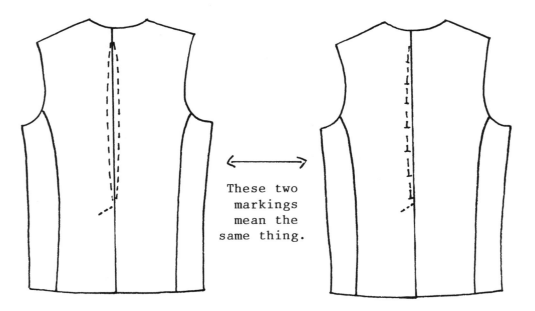

These two
markings
mean the
same thing.

Chalk marks mean "take
in" the CB seam.

Pins mean "take in" the
CB seam.

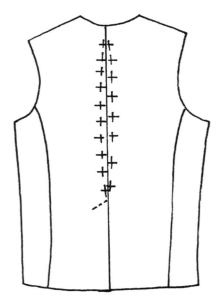

These chalk marks mean
"let out this much."

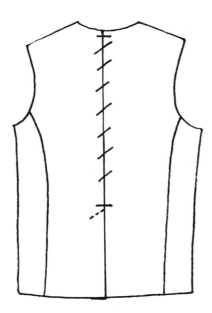

The horizontal lines at
the top and bottom mean "stop
here." The diagonal slashes
mean "let out all possible."

12

It is a good idea to make your conversation consistent and explicit by referring to making a garment smaller as "taking in," and to making a garment larger as "letting out." For hems, always use "shorten" or "lengthen" and there will be no mistake as to what is meant. These are used instead of expressions like "taking up," which could mean either shortening the hem or taking the sides in.

The use of chalk is also very helpful when transferring markings from the outside to the inside of the garment. Let's assume you are taking in the sideseams of a coat. You have pinned it and now must transfer your pin marks to the inside so you will be able to sew.

Go to the inside of the garment and make small chalk marks just where the pins are holding the fabric together. Remove the pins and connect the marks forming a solid line. This will signify the new sewing line.

If there are only chalk marks and no pins on the garment, go to the inside and put chalk marks directly under the ones on the outside. Do this by pressing down on each mark with your finger from the outside and pressing up from the inside with chalk. Connect the marks and sew.

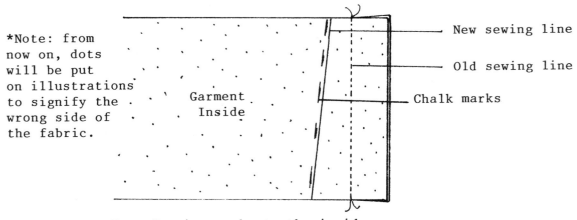

*Note: from now on, dots will be put on illustrations to signify the wrong side of the fabric.

Garment Inside

New sewing line

Old sewing line

Chalk marks

Transferring marks to the inside.

When a garment is pinned on a customer, it won't be as tight as if there were a complete seam sewn. Because of this, always sew on the outside of your new sewing line (don't take it in as much) when taking in. This will guard against "over altering," a common mistake among novice alterationists. In like manner, if you are shortening a pair of pants or sleeves, always make them a fraction longer than you have marked them because they will "draw up" or shorten slightly as the customer wears them.

After fitting, marking, and sewing, the time comes for ripping out. I often hear the complaint, "If it weren't for the ripping out, I'd love to sew!" My answer is, "Learn an easy way to rip out!" Traditional seam rippers are never used in tailoring shops but are replaced by single-edged razor blades, and sometimes by small pocket knives. Using a sharp razor blade or knife appears to be much riskier than using a seam ripper; but in actuality, it is not. How many times have you torn the fabric or cut your hand by trying to force a dull seam ripper? All you need is practice and I am sure you will be amazed at the speed you will develop in ripping. Incidentally, the best place to buy razor blades in bulk is at a home improvement or paint store.

Take advantage of chain stitches and blindhem stitches which are sewn with one or two continuous threads. They will always rip out quickly by clipping a few threads and pulling from left to right. In general, always sew the new seam before ripping out the old one. The old seam will serve to replace basting or pinning while you're sewing the new one.

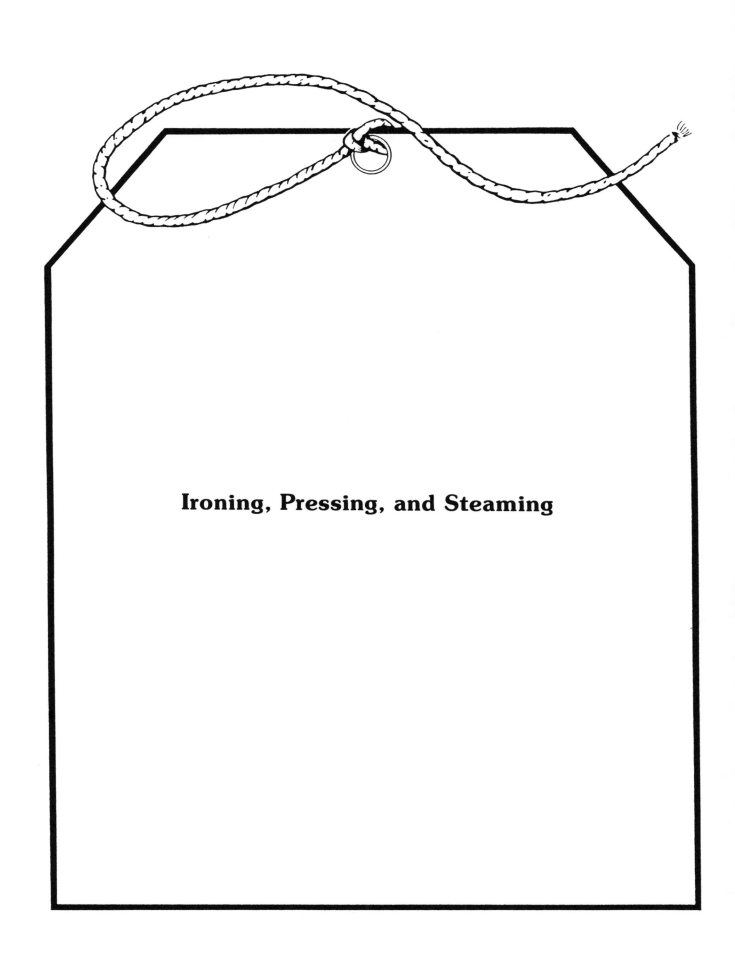

Ironing, Pressing, and Steaming

Pressing in men's alterations is equally important with fitting and sewing. You will need to develop an expertise with whatever pressing equipment you use. This is essential in order to achieve a finished look in any garment.

With your common household iron, you will be able to perform most tasks, if you learn to use it properly. With it you will be able to iron, press, and steam. There is a distinct difference between these procedures.

Ironing is the process which is used mostly for removing wrinkles from entire garments or from large areas of garments. It can be done with a dry iron or with steam. A minimum of pressure is used and the iron is slid back and forth. To avoid wrinkling during the process, iron detailed areas first and then the larger areas.

Ironing

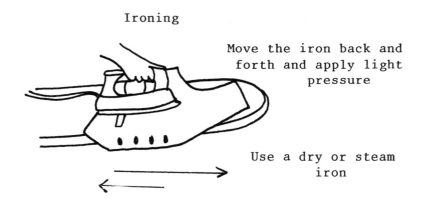

Move the iron back and forth and apply light pressure

Use a dry or steam iron

Pressing is used mostly in tailoring and is done by applying heat, moisture, and pressure to small areas of the garment at a time. It is used for molding, shaping, and permanently setting parts of the garment into place.

Pressing can either be "hard" or "soft." A hard press is used to form a crease, as in pants. A soft press is used to make a soft fold, such as in the edges of a necktie.

Because the iron is put directly on the fabric and force is applied, always use a press cloth unless you have tested your fabric carefully beforehand.

Pressing is used to fuse interfacing to fabric, and on small areas of the garment, because the iron stays in one place instead of sliding back and forth.

Allow garments and garment parts to cool in the position they were pressed. It is the same principle as electric rollers. After using heat and moisture, the pressed area is allowed to become cool and dry, and the press is set.

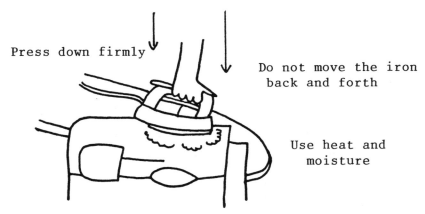

Press down firmly

Do not move the iron
back and forth

Use heat and
moisture

Pressing

Steaming is done by holding the iron away from the fabric and allowing the steam to penetrate the garment. This process is used to ease or shrink fabric in such areas as the sleeve cap. Steaming can also be used to remove wrinkles from napped fabrics or to restore the nap if it has been flattened. A "shot-of-steam" iron works well for steaming because the flow of steam can be regulated.

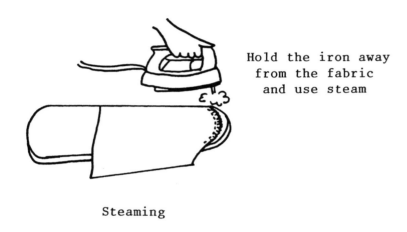

Hold the iron away from the fabric and use steam

Steaming

Ironing the customer's garment will be much easier if you use a pressing table instead of an ironing board. The ideal table can be made cheaply by padding and covering a door and positioning it on a table, dresser, bookcases, or other sturdy support. The stability and added surface size will give you the strength you need for pressing and the area you need for the garment, iron, and other accessories. If you don't have enough space for a whole door, cover and pad as large a board as possible.

Your pressing area should include a squirt bottle, several press cloths, a seam gauge, and a ruler.

A sleeve board is an absolute necessity when doing men's alterations. Not only can you press sleeves and shoulders, you can press pant seams, shirt sleeves, and many other garment parts. The kinds that are not collapsible are sturdier. You may save money by purchasing one and covering it yourself.

A pressing ham is also indispensable and is used for pressing curved areas. A ham is covered on one side with wool and on the other side with cotton. The wool side is used for wool and napped fabrics and the cotton side is for most others.

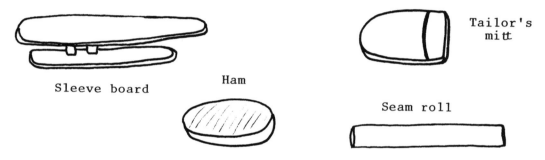

Sleeve board   Ham   Tailor's mitt   Seam roll

A seam roll is used for pressing seams, especially when they might leave a mark on the right side of the garment. I find that putting heavy brown paper under the seam allowances works well for this also.

A tailor's mitt has a pocket on one side for your hand. You can use it to press hard-to-get-at areas that need support underneath, but can't be slipped onto a sleeve board or ironing board. The thick mitt keeps you from burning your hand. You can also use it to pound out steam and to put in the hem of a sleeve when pressing. This keeps a crease from being pressed into the sides of the sleeve hem.

19

There are always areas that these commercial aids don't fit into, so I keep a towel handy and fold it to fit the specific area.

A tailor's clapper or pounding block is used to clap or pound the steam out of an area you have just pressed. It is held in place until the area is cool, thus setting the press.

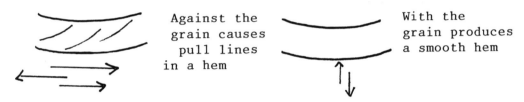 Tailor's clapper or pounding block

Following are some general tips for pressing:

*   Press seams together before pressing them open. This reduces puckering when the seam is pressed open.
*   Press with the grain of the fabric. Pressing against the grain or at an angle causes distortion.

Against the grain causes pull lines in a hem

With the grain produces a smooth hem

*   Never press over stains or dirt because heat will set the stain.
*   Never press over pins. You may make a permanent dent in the fabric and you may scratch the bottom of the iron.
*   Always let the garment or area you have pressed become dry before moving it. This sets the press.
*   To raise the nap on a fabric, steam it first. Then rub the fabric briskly, but gently on itself. Continue until the nap is raised.

PRESSING WHILE YOU WAIT!

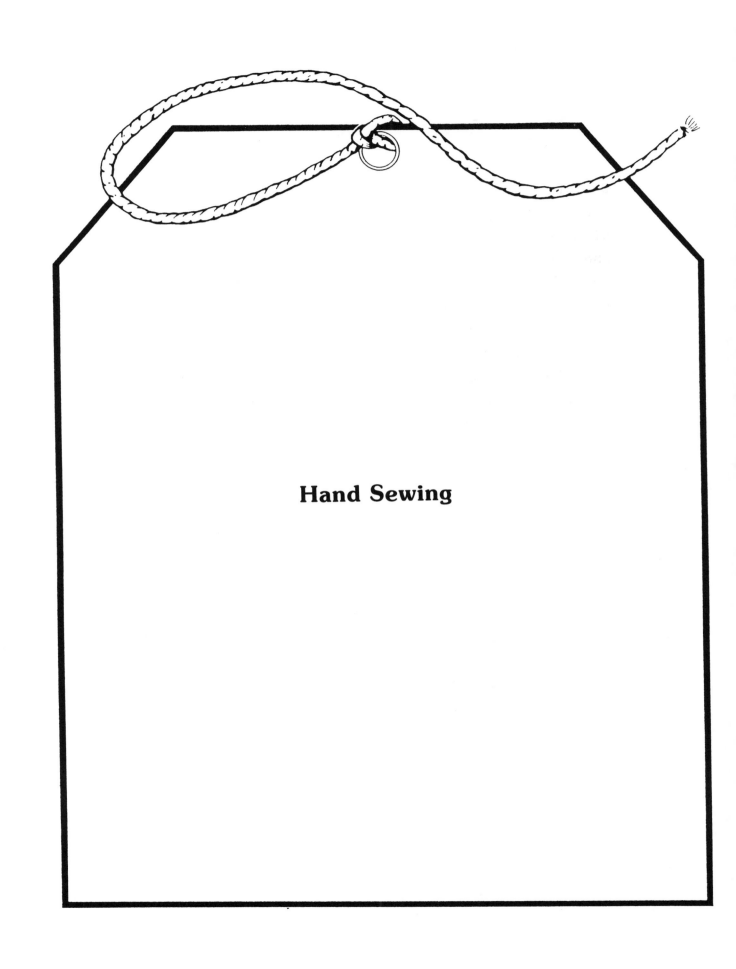

Hand Sewing

Basting

Basting is a temporary stitch used to hold alterations in place for a second or final fitting. Basting is better than pinning after the first fitting because it will allow the garment a smooth finish and the customer will not be stuck with pins when he views the garment. Basting is usually done on a flat surface and with a thread length longer than the norm. Start with one or two small backstitches instead of a knot and continue with a long running stitch going in and out of the fabric at one half inch intervals. (Stitches may be as long as 1½".) A knot is not used so the basting can be easily removed if needed.

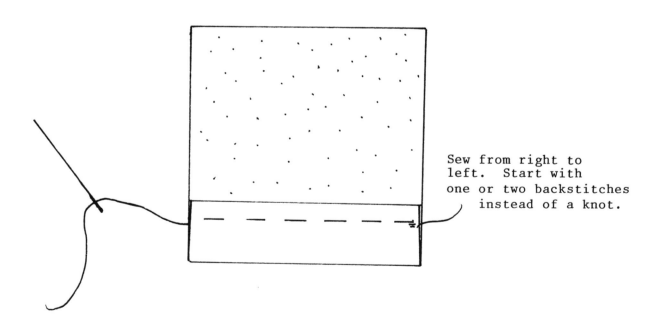

Sew from right to left. Start with one or two backstitches instead of a knot.

Running Stitch

   A running stitch is a stitch similar to basting, only smaller and permanent. It is used for tacking lining to the bottom of jacket sleeves or hems and for tacking down facing. A running stitch with a double thread is used for shrinking lapels.

   Sewing from right to left, use a regular length of thread with a knot and a small stitch, about one fourth inch or less. Weave back and forth or in and out as needed. Make sure the stitches do not show on the outside of the garment.

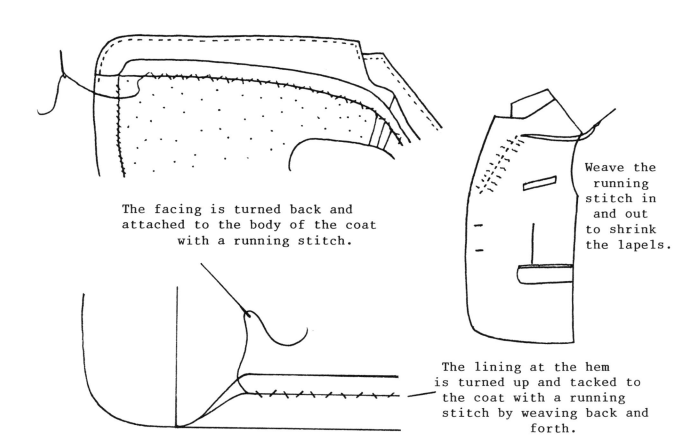

The facing is turned back and
attached to the body of the coat
with a running stitch.

Weave the
running
stitch in
and out
to shrink
the lapels.

The lining at the hem
is turned up and tacked to
the coat with a running
stitch by weaving back and
forth.

Whip Stitch

The whip stitch is also called the overcast stitch which describes it perfectly. It was originally used to finish edges of fabric before we had zig-zag machine stitches or sergers. How time-consuming that must have been!

Now, the whip stitch is used quite often for hems and in many other instances where fabric needs to be "whipped" together.

Use a single thread and make the stitches small and even. Sew from right to left.

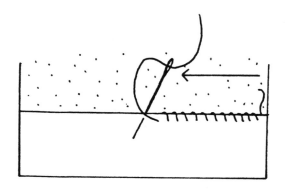

Sew from right to left.

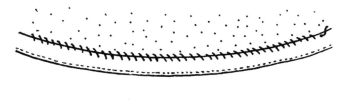

Whip stitch used to hem a skirt after tape has been applied

Prick Stitch

The prick stitch is sometimes known as the pick stitch or the back stitch. It was originally used to sew seams before the invention of the sewing machine because it is so durable. Now it is used mostly for decorative purposes and usually in tailored garments.

In women's clothing, the prick stitch is often used for applying zippers. In men's clothing, it is used almost exclusively for topstitching.

You will see this stitch done with a single thread, but I prefer to use a double thread for strength. Silk topstitching thread is quite often used because it enhances the appearance and does not tangle.

Working on the right side of the fabric, come from the wrong side (or from inside layers of the fabric), up and out. Depending on the length of stitch desired, go back into the fabric behind the point where you first came up. Surface again ahead of the original opening. Keep your stitches even and in a straight line.

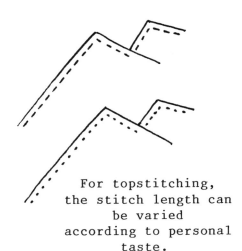

For topstitching, the stitch length can be varied according to personal taste.

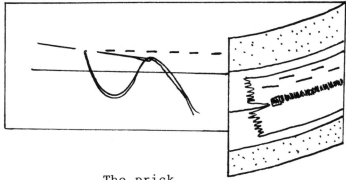

The prick stitch used to apply a zipper.

Catch Stitch

The catch stitch is probably the stitch most readily recognized as a tailoring stitch because it is so distinctive.

It is quite often used for hems, but should only be used for this purpose when the hem is covered by lining. This is because most of the thread which forms the stitch is exposed and vulnerable to friction (such as the shoe rubbing against the hem in pants), which eventually will cause the thread to wear and break.

The catch stitch is used for its aesthetic appeal in attaching labels and for securing pleats in lining.

Use a single thread and sew from left to right. Keep the stitches firm but not tight.

Sew from left to right

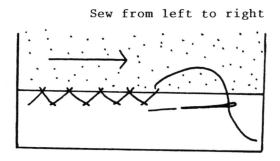

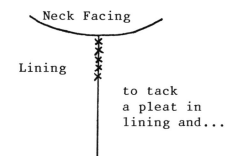

Use the catch
stitch to attach
labels and...

to tack
a pleat in
lining and...

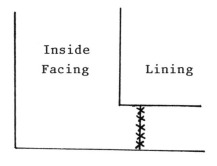

to tack the facing
edge at the hem of a coat.

Felling

This stitch and the process of doing the stitch are both called felling. The felling stitch is used in finishing and has a few variations.

When it is used to fasten sleeve lining around the armholes in a coat, the stitch is concealed. This prevents friction (such as the arm rubbing on the lining) from wearing through the thread. You can also fell in this manner when stitching new lining around the inside pocket welts when relining.

Felling is used in another way when attaching the undercollar to the coat and upper collar. The stitches show and are at right angles.

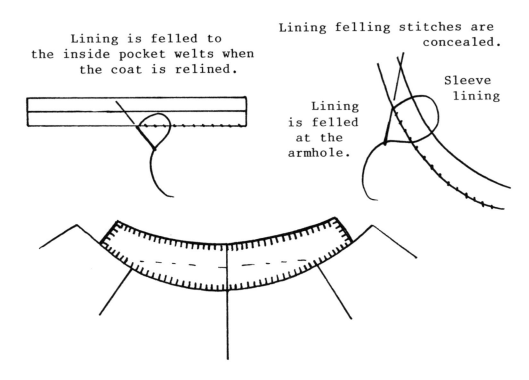

Lining is felled to the inside pocket welts when the coat is relined.

Lining felling stitches are concealed.

Sleeve lining

Lining is felled at the armhole.

The undercollar is felled with obvious perpendicular stitches.

Buttons

Under the category of hand sewing, I would like to review the steps in sewing a button on because they are so important, and because you will be asked to do this seemingly simple job many times. Buttons for shirts are sewn on with a beeswax reinforced double strand of regular thread. Increase to buttonhole twist, heavy duty thread, or carpet thread for pants, vests, and coats.

Every button, except decorative ones (like the ones on sleeves or the left side of a double-breasted coat), must have a shank for strength and to work properly. If the button does not have a built-in shank, you can form one easily by putting a needle, toothpick, or match on top of the button and sewing over it. After you have removed the aid, wind the thread around the shank several times and tie it off.

Try not to cut corners by applying buttons on the machine. You cannot properly form a shank this way and the stitching almost always unravels.

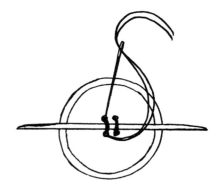

Put the toothpick
between the stitching and
the button.

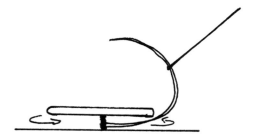

Remove the toothpick and
twist the thread around
the stitches to form the
shank.

Buttonholes

You may need to replace an imitation buttonhole like the ones on sleeves or lapels. You may also be asked to "hand work" a functioning buttonhole in a new garment or in one that needs repair. Using buttonhole twist, follow the steps below for each.

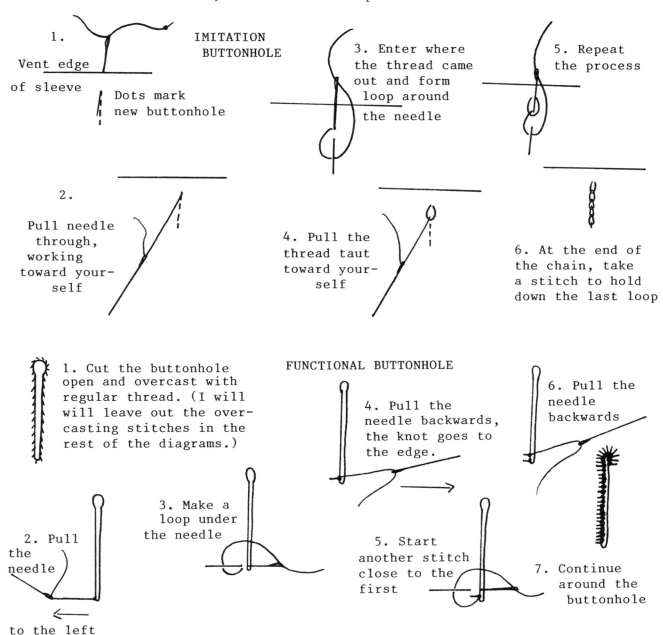

1.
Vent edge
of sleeve

IMITATION
BUTTONHOLE

Dots mark
new buttonhole

3. Enter where
the thread came
out and form
loop around
the needle

5. Repeat
the process

2.
Pull needle
through,
working
toward your-
self

4. Pull the
thread taut
toward your-
self

6. At the end of
the chain, take
a stitch to hold
down the last loop

1. Cut the buttonhole
open and overcast with
regular thread. (I will
will leave out the over-
casting stitches in the
rest of the diagrams.)

FUNCTIONAL BUTTONHOLE

4. Pull the
needle backwards,
the knot goes to
the edge.

6. Pull the
needle
backwards

3. Make a
loop under
the needle

2. Pull
the
needle

5. Start
another stitch
close to the
first

7. Continue
around the
buttonhole

to the left

29

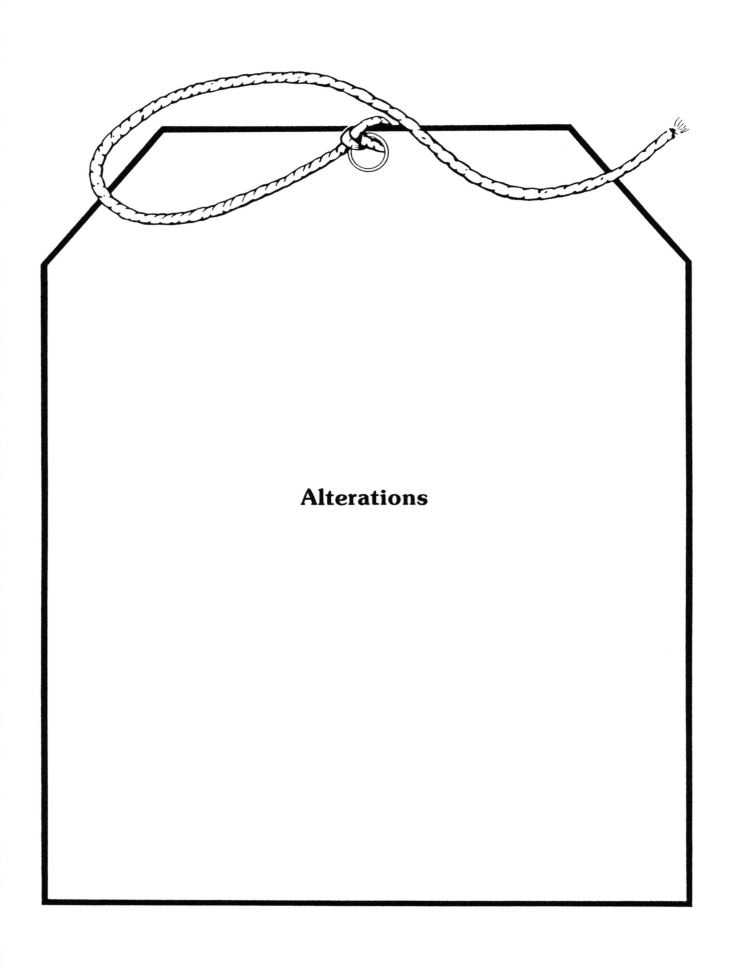

Alterations

It is now time to turn to instructions for each individual alteration. I have tried to include every common alteration as well as some that are not so common. No matter how inclusive the list, there will always be some new style or construction method which you will have to figure out yourself. This is when you will use the garment itself for your teacher. Examine how it was sewn originally and put it back together the same way. Do this by taking notes if necessary. Also, do one side at a time. Then you will have the undone side to refer to.

Sometimes, because you have no choice, you will have to develop your own procedure. In this case, try not to slash or trim your seam allowances or hems until you are sure the alteration is fitted properly. If you have to trim fabric in order for the garment to lay properly, such as when mitering corners, be sure the customer knows in advance that the alteration is irreversible. The ability to be flexible and creative is what makes a good alterationist.

"BUT I ONLY HAVE ENOUGH FOOD FOR 2 WEEKS!!"

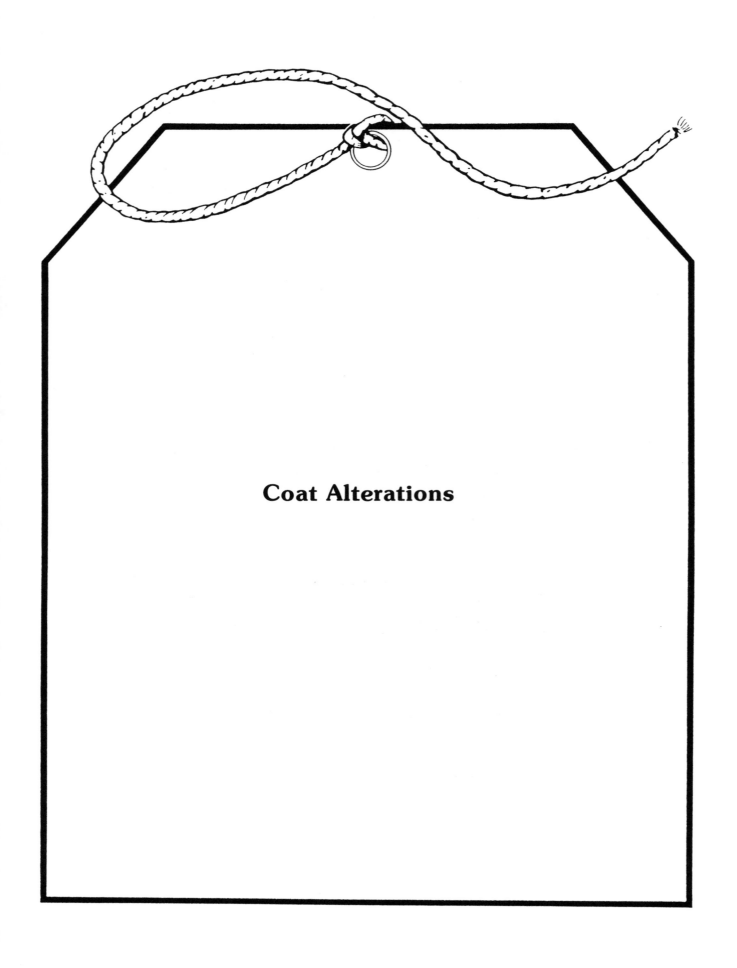

Coat Alterations

Sleeves

Shortening Sleeves without Vents

When you have determined the desired length of the sleeve, fold it under and mark it with chalk, or measure the amount to be lengthened. Whenever marking a sleeve hem, make it a little longer than measured (whether lengthening or shortening), because the sleeve will "draw up" after wearing.

With all sleeves, do one first and use the other as a guide.

1. Draw a continuous chalk mark around the sleeve on the new hemline. Measure the amount to be shortened and make a record of it. This can be done easily with an adjustable seam gauge.

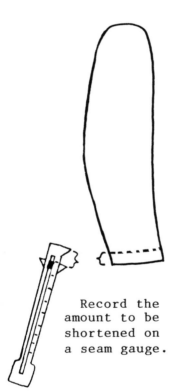

Record the amount to be shortened on a seam gauge.

*The sleeves on men's overcoats will probably be the only ones in men's clothing without vents. Be sure to fit an overcoat over the customer's suit coat and make the overcoat sleeves at least ½" longer.

2. Remove buttons if there are any.

3. Rip the lining and the old hem.

4. If the sleeves are shortened more than ½", move the interfacing up.

5. Press the hem up and trim any excess fabric. Sew the hem, lining, and buttons (details for all three are in "Hand Sewing").

6. Give the hem a final press. To avoid pressing a lengthwise crease in the sleeve, fold a towel so it fits snugly in the sleeve. Pressing mits are made for this purpose, but I prefer a towel so it can be folded to fit any size. Insert the towel into the sleeve in the same position the customer's arm would be in.

Never press a crease in the sleeve.

Use a rolled towel to press the hem.

*If the sleeves were shortened a lot, they may be too wide at the bottom and must be narrowed before the hem is sewn. Refer to " Narrowing Sleeves" for details.

Shortening Sleeves with Vents

1. Mark the new hemline all around and remove the buttons.

2. Rip the lining from the hem and rip the hem. If you are shortening more than ½", move the lining up. If the lining is fused in place, fuse more above it rather than trying to remove it.

3. Following are the directions for mitering:

a. On the inside, draw the new hemline.

b. Draw a chalk line on the fold line of the vent.

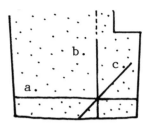

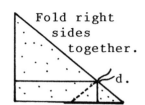
Fold right sides together.

c. Draw a 45° diagonal line through the intersection of lines a and b.

d. Fold the diagonal line together and stitch.

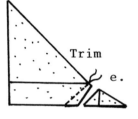
Trim

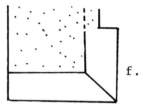

e. Trim close to the seam.

f. Turn and press.

Inside

4. Shorten the unmitered corner on the machine just as it had been done originally.

5. Tack the hem up at the seamline.

6. Fold the lining up the amount you shortened the sleeve and press it.

7. Pin the mitered vent together.

8. Tack the lining to the sleeve.

9. Resew the buttons.

10. Press as described in "Shortening Sleeves without Vents."

*If the sleeve is shortened so much that there is not enough fabric to make a vent, sew the vented seam together and shorten it as if it were a sleeve with no vent.

Lengthening Sleeves

Men's clothing almost always has large hems for lengthening. In addition, the mitered corners are not trimmed as a rule, which allows you to lengthen them easily. If you find that there is enough fabric, follow the previous directions, but lengthen when needed.

When adding a facing to sleeves, sometimes it is less bulky and looks better if you add to the lining rather than to the sleeve. It is easier to match the lining fabric than the outer fabric. If you do this, be sure to add interfacing to the bottom of the sleeve for more body.

If you are lengthening a sleeve all possible, you may have to take in the underarm seam at the bottom slightly. The sleeve has been made wider at the bottom so the hem will fit the sleeve when turned up.

After you have straightened the seam, you can do the hem as usual. Don't forget to straighten the lining too.

If you add a facing to the sleeve, angle it outward at the top so it will fit when turned up. It's best to use a bias facing and very important not to stretch it or the sleeve during application.

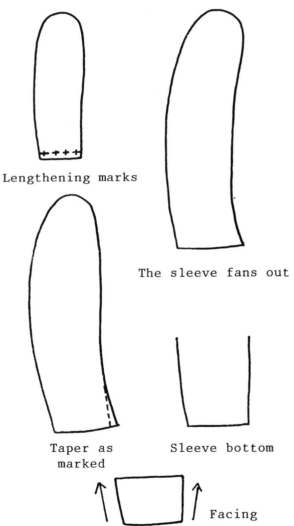

Lengthening marks

The sleeve fans out

Taper as marked

Sleeve bottom

Facing

36

Shortening or Lengthening Raincoat Sleeves

Fit the raincoat over the customer's suit so you will be sure to get the raincoat sleeves at least ½" longer.

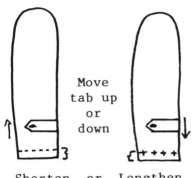

Move tab up or down

Shorten   or   Lengthen

1. Measure the amount the hem is to be changed and record it on a seam gauge. Be very careful with chalk marks on raincoat fabric.

2. Before altering the hem, you must move the tabs. Turn the sleeve inside out and look for a seam in the lining that has been topstitched together. Rip it open. If there isn't evidence of one, rip open about 5" of the back sleeve seam (or under-arm seam) in the elbow area.

Topstitched lining seam

3. Pull the sleeve inside out through the hole. Rip the seam where the tab is inserted and move it up or down the amount the hem is being altered.

4. Rip out any threads that are tacking up the hem.

Rip open the seam

5. Find the sewing line where the lining is attached to the bottom of the sleeve. Measure up or down from the seam the amount to be altered. Sew on your new line. (If lengthening, you may need to face at this point.) You will be sewing around a tube. If shortening   more than ½", move the interfacing.

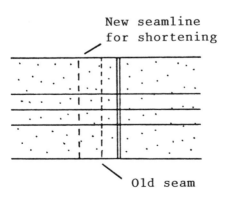

New seamline for shortening

Old seam

37

6. Trim the excess fabric.

7. Turn the sleeve right side out. The lining will automatically pull the hem up. Press on the new hemline, turning all seam allowances upward. Tack the hem in place at the seamlines.

Narrowing Sleeves

If you are narrowing sleeves, remember they must fit over other garments and still have ease. Fit the customer when he has on other clothing he will be wearing under the coat.

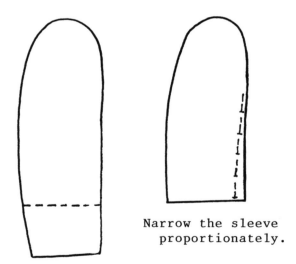

Vertical ripples mean the sleeve is too wide.

Pin as needed.

Another reason for narrowing coat sleeves is caused when sleeves are shortened excessively. This brings the hemline up to a wider point in the sleeve.

Pin out the excess fabric and alter on the underarm seam. Go to nothing at the armhole.

Narrow the sleeve proportionately.

The sleeve needs to be shortened excessively.

Correcting Sleeve Pitch

Incorrect sleeve pitch will cause diagonal pull lines to form in the caps of the sleeves. Because this is hard to fit, you may want to remove the sleeve and actually "hang" or "set" it on the customer by pinning it in place. The shoulder dot and other sleeve placement markings will not match after rotation. The average amount to rotate a sleeve in coats is 1". If you are rotating less than this amount, you may need to rotate the cap of the sleeves only. In either case, the shoulder pad stays in the same position and the sleeve head rotates with the sleeve. See "Narrowing Shoulders" for more details on armholes. Rotate the lining accordingly.

If the lines are on the front, the sleeve cap needs to be rotated toward the front.

If the lines are on the back, the sleeve cap needs to be rotated toward the back.

As you become more experienced with this problem, you will be able to put a pin in the sleeve cap that indicates where the new shoulder dot should be. In other words, when the sleeve is rotated, the pin will match up to the shoulder seam.

Rotate the sleeve forward.

Rotate the sleeve backward.

This sleeve hangs too far forward.

Dotted lines show the correct sleeve pitch.

This sleeve hangs backward.

Sideseams

In or Out with a Center Back Vent

Where women's coats are usually taken in or let out on the sideseams, men's coats are always altered on the side back seams.

For fitting, have the customer button the top button, and put a pin in the vent to hold it together. Proceed to mark the side back seams for taking in or letting out.

Transfer the marks to the inside and alter as needed. Alter the lining in the same way.

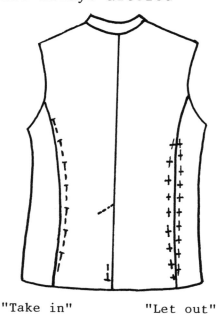

"Take in"   "Let out"

In or Out with Double Vents

Some disreputable tailors will try to save time by altering on the CB seam when there are double vents. This pulls the sideback seams inward and throws them off-grain, and for that reason, is not recommended.

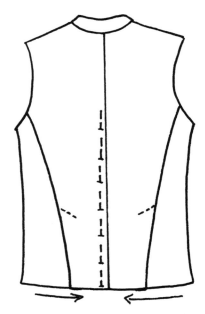

Taking in the CB seam pulls the sideseams inward and throws them off-grain.

40

For fitting, have the customer button the top button in front, and pin the two back vents closed. Mark for letting out or pin for taking in. Where the vents are pinned shut, treat the seam as if it were sewn together and pin accordingly.

1. Transfer markings to the inside. When taking in, sew to the top of the vent.

2. Rip the stitching across the top of the vent. Rip the outer flap of the vent (the one that is folded under) at the hem and anywhere it is tacked down. Do not rip the lining from the vent.

3. Fold the vent inward the amount the seam was taken in. It will want to do this naturally. If you're letting out, make the fold shallower.

4. The inner flap of the vent is not altered. Do the other side. Alter lining accordingly. If you are letting out all possible, you may let out the CB seam too.

5. Topstitch across the tops of the vents if they were done before.

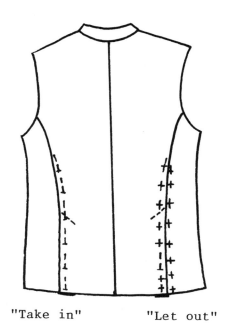

"Take in"   "Let out"

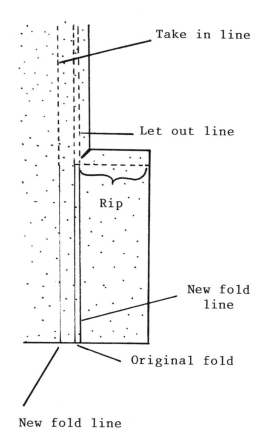

Take in line

Let out line

Rip

New fold line

Original fold

New fold line

41

Sideseams into Armholes

Taking In

When the seams need to be taken in all the way into the armholes, you will have to drop the armholes to compensate.

The natural tendency would be to take in the sleeves to fit the smaller armholes, but this would make the sleeves too tight.

Instead, rip the bottom half of the sleeves from the armholes. Take in the sideseams first and then reapply the sleeves on the new lower sewing lines. To determine where the new lines will be, pin in the sleeves to see where they will fit.

Trim the fabric from the armholes where you have dropped them, or they will feel too tight. Alter the lining in the same way.

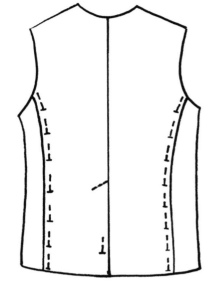

Sideseams pinned into armholes.

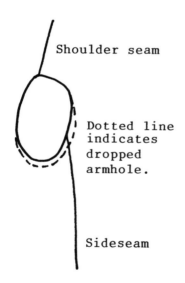

Shoulder seam

Dotted line indicates dropped armhole.

Sideseam

Letting Out

When letting out, let out the back sleeve seams all possible at the top so the sleeves will be big enough for the body of the coat.

Center Back Seam

Taking In

Vertical folds will appear at the back of the coat over the shoulder blades.

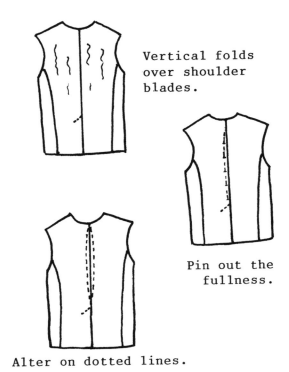

Vertical folds over shoulder blades.

1. Pin out the excess.

2. If the total amount is 1" or less, alter as indicated by taking in on the dotted lines. Make a smooth line, going to nothing gradually.

Pin out the fullness.

Alter on dotted lines.

3. If the total amount is more than 1", pin 1" total out of the CB seam first.

Then pin a ridge of fabric as needed along the armhole and out of the <u>back</u> of the side back seam only.

Pin just enough to remove the extra fabric, but not enough to hinder movement.

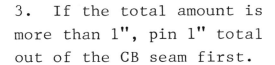

Pin 1" total out of CB and remove the rest of the fullness from the arm-hole and back of the side-back seam.

4. Alter as indicated on the dotted lines. You will have to remove the back of the sleeve down to the underarm.

It is very uncommon to remove this much, but if you do, charge accordingly.

Letting Out

Horizontal lines will form across the shoulder blades and the customer will inevitably complain that the coat is "too tight across the shoulders."

1. If the coat is not extremely tight, let out the CB seam all possible. Taper to nothing gradually.

2. If the coat is quite tight, let out the CB seam all possible and let out the upper side back seam on the back only.

3. Let out as indicated by the dotted lines.

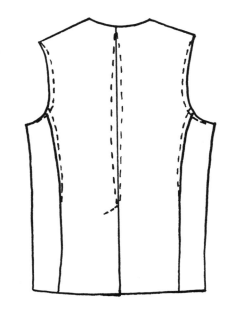

Alter on dotted lines.

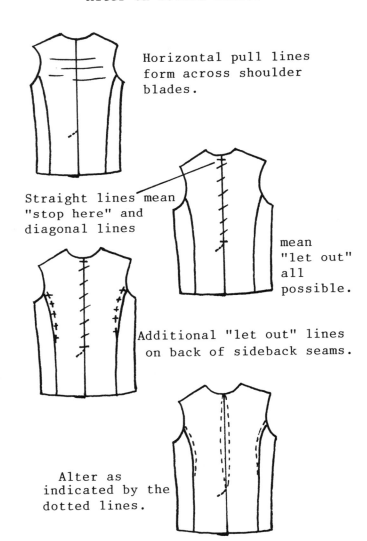

Horizontal pull lines form across shoulder blades.

Straight lines mean "stop here" and diagonal lines

mean "let out" all possible.

Additional "let out" lines on back of sideback seams.

Alter as indicated by the dotted lines.

44

The front darts may be taken
in or let out as needed.
Some coats are cut with underarm darts which can also be
altered.

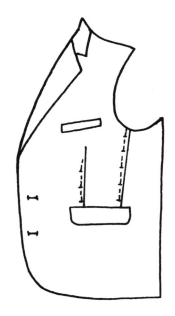

Because these areas are hard
to reach inside the coat, and
alterations produce negligible
results, try to do all the
altering on the seamlines first.

Front dart and underarm
dart pinned.

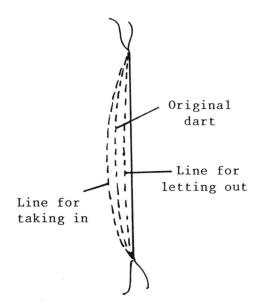

Original
dart

Line for
letting out

Line for
taking in

When altering darts, make smooth
seams and taper to the points
gradually. Always alter the
lining accordingly.

Narrowing Shoulders

Narrowing shoulders in a coat is considered a major alteration because it involves lining, shoulder pads, sleeve heads, and the sleeve seam.

Because of this, men are always advised to purchase a coat that fits well in the shoulders and have it altered in the sides or sleeves.

Surprisingly enough, if a man has lost weight, he may need to have the shoulders narrowed. Men carry the majority of their weight in their upper bodies (women are the opposite), so this is where weight loss is significant.

1. Draw a chalk line on the shoulders signifying the new sewing line.

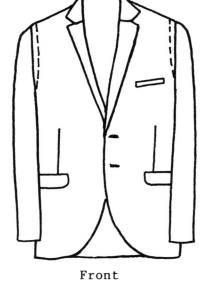

Front

2. Rip the lining and study how the shoulder pad and sleeve head are inserted. I advise completing one side first, using the other as a guide.

Back

46

The illustration below shows the shoulder pad
and sleeve head. In men's clothing they are sewn in
by hand because a home sewing machine could not sew
through all the layers.

The seams in the armscye (bottom half of the armhole) are trimmed and not pressed open. The seams in
the sleeve cap (top half of the armhole) are pressed
open and sandwiched between the shoulder pad and the
sleeve head.

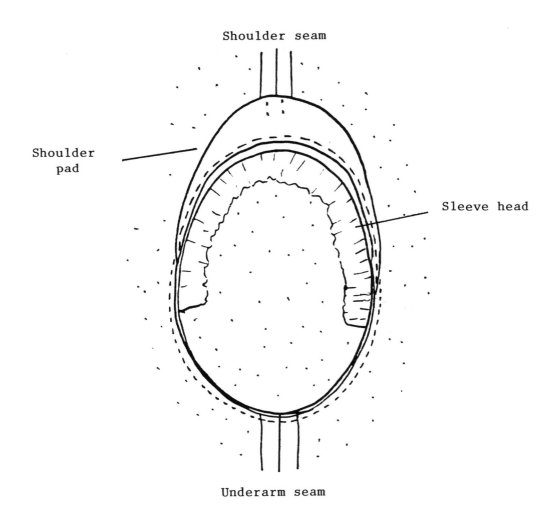

Shoulder seam

Shoulder
pad

Sleeve head

Underarm seam

3. Rip the pad and sleeve head. Pin the sleeve head to the sleeve cap loosely to mark its position.

4. Rip the sleeve seam in the area of the alteration.

5. Trim the shoulder seam to within 3/8" of the new sewing line.

6. Resew the cap of the sleeve and press the seam open.

7. Reapply the shoulder pad, sleeve head, and lining (see "Hand Sewing" for the lining stitch).

8. Press on a sleeve board.

*If you narrow the shoulders more than 3/4", you will have to remove the entire sleeve and take in the side back seam or the underarm dart on the coat. This is because narrowing the shoulders causes the armhole to become larger, and the sleeve will no longer be big enough to fit it. Before removing the sleeve, mark where it connects to the armhole. Remove the sleeve and trim the excess from the shoulder. To determine how much to take in the seams, pin the sleeves at the shoulders, fronts, and backs. As you pin down to the underarm, you will see how much the seam needs to be altered.

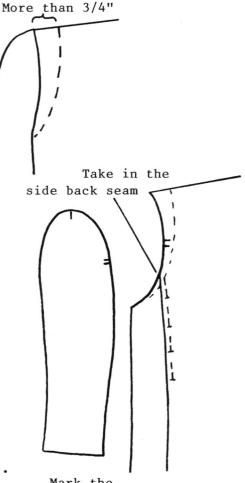

More than 3/4"

Take in the side back seam

Mark the sleeve at one or more places

Dropping Shoulders

When the shoulders need to
be dropped, diagonal lines
form on the coat from the
shoulders to the armholes.
Sometimes this will occur
in only one shoulder.

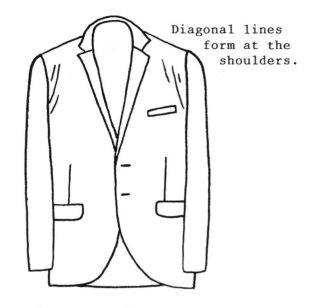

Diagonal lines
form at the
shoulders.

Since dropping shoulders
is a major alteration,
first try adding shoulder
pads. For fitting, put
the pad between the coat
and the customer's shoul-
der to see if the lines
disappear. If they do,
rip the sleeve cap of the
lining and insert the new
pad on top of the orig-
inal one. Sew it in by
hand and fell the lining
as described in the "Hand
Sewing" section.

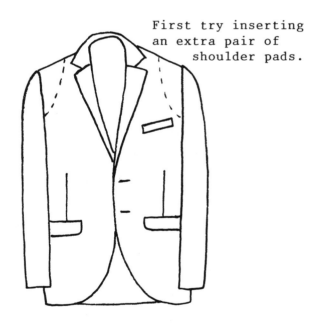

First try inserting
an extra pair of
shoulder pads.

If the addition of shoul-
der pads does not correct
the problem, you must drop
the shoulders.

Grasp the shoulder seam and "pick up the shoulders" until the lines disappear. Because of the shoulder pads, it will be hard to pin out the excess, so mark on each side of the seam with chalk. Go to nothing at the neck.

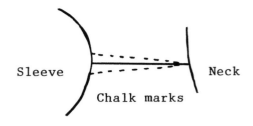

Mark the sleeve where it attaches at the shoulder and underarm. Then remove the entire sleeve and sleeve lining from the coat. Remove the shoulder pad and sleeve head. Take in the shoulder seam as marked.

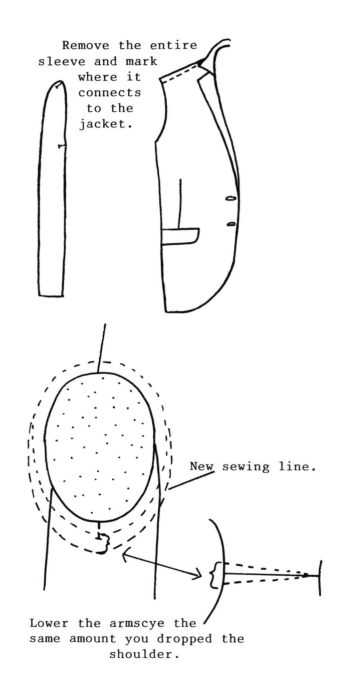

Because taking in the shoulder seam makes the armhole lower, you must lower the armscye (bottom half of the armhole) the same amount. Baste on the new sewing line and trim the seam.

Replace the shoulder pad and sleeve head. Resew the sleeve and lining, matching the marks. The notches on the sides of the armhole will no longer match.

Shortening a Coat

1. Mark the new hemline all around.

2. Detach the lining if there is one, and rip the old hem out.

3. If there is topstitching on the CF, rip it out high enough so it is out of your work area.

4. Transfer the markings to the inside. If the coat is curved in the front (the only ones not curved will probably be overcoats), turn the facing inside out. Use one side as a pattern to copy the curve outline on the other side.

5. Sew the new curve and trim it. To make a smooth curve, trim close to the edge with pinking shears.

If the bottom is straight at the CF, do one side at a time and duplicate the way it was originally trimmed and pressed. To eliminate bulk at the bottom corners, trim close to the seams where the hem folds up. You can also stitch the ditch of the facing seam before the facing is folded back.

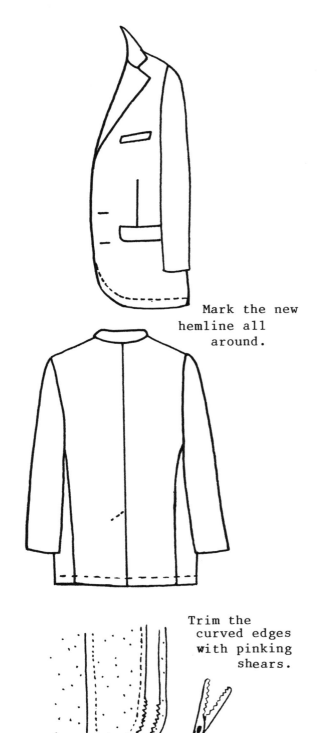

Mark the new hemline all around.

Trim the curved edges with pinking shears.

51

There are several different
ways the lining may meet up
with the bottom of the facing. Use the original way
it was done as your guide.

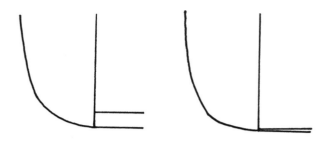

The lining is up
from the bottom.

The lining is
flush.

To make the lining flush
with the bottom, sew the
curve and stop 1" from the
edge of the facing.

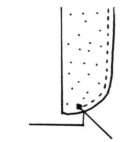

Stop sewing 1" from the edge
of the facing.

Sew the bottom of the lining
to the facing, right sides
together. Sew the lining as
far as it will go to the 1"
of facing that was left undone.

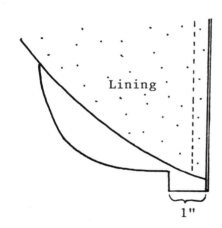

Lining

1"

Turn the 1" flap under.
The lining automatically
turns under with it and
will be flush with the
bottom.

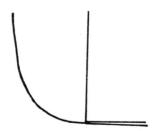

The lining is flush
with the bottom.

If you want the lining to
stop above the hemline of
the coat, turn the lining
up ½" before stitching it
to the facing. In this instance, you can sew the
facing curve all the way.

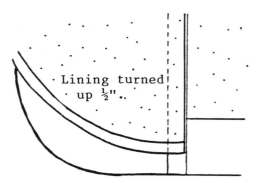
Lining turned
up ½"..

Turn the lining right side
out and press seams toward
the lining, except for the
facing that is below the
lining.

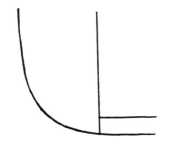
Clip
and turn
under.

Clip the facing at the bottom of the lining, and turn
the raw edge under. Tack it
in place.

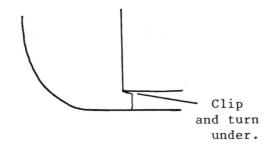

Lining is up from the
bottom.

For overcoats, the fabric may
be too bulky to turn under.
Leave the raw edge and make
a small row of the tailor's
catch stitch over it ("Hand
Sewing" chapter).

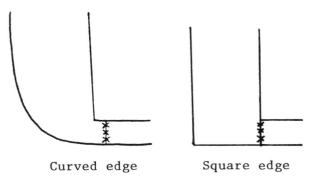

Curved edge   Square edge

53

6. Turn the new hem up and press it. Move the inter-facing up if necessary.

7. Sew the hem using one of the stitches described in the "Hand Sewing" chapter.

8. Turn the lining under and press it. Trim if there is more than 1" turned under. Always pin the lining down and check the outside to see if it is pulling.

9. There should be some give or play at the bottom of the lining. Turn it up ¼" and tack it to the jacket with a running stitch. Resew the lining to the vent.

10. Press the hem and replace the topstitching. If you cannot match the thread in color or thickness, you may have to remove all the topstitching from the collar, lapels, and the CF edge. Then replace it all with the same thread.

Shortening a Raincoat

As with coats, there are many different hemming styles or techniques, and you will need to duplicate the original one.

Raincoat hems are almost always topstitched, and matching the thread can be very difficult. Advise the customer that he may have to settle for the best possible match.

Be careful when marking. Wax chalk almost always leaves a grease mark on raincoat fabric, and pins quite often leave permanent holes. A light mark with real chalk is the best.

A raincoat hem is one of the few hems that is folded over twice and topstitched. Give the hem a good press before sewing. Raincoat fabric does not ease in well. If you find there is excess fabric which does not allow the hem to lie flat, you may need to take in each seam below the hemline.

To reduce bulk at the front corners, you can trim the facing corner before sewing.

To attach lining to the edge of the pleat, first sew the lining hem. The lining is ripped from the pleat at the bottom so you can do this. This is done before the hem is sewn down.

Fold the lining and coat right sides together and stitch them at the bottom.

Fold the hem up on the hemline, sandwiching the lining between the hem and the edge of the pleat. Stitch. Turn to the right side and press.

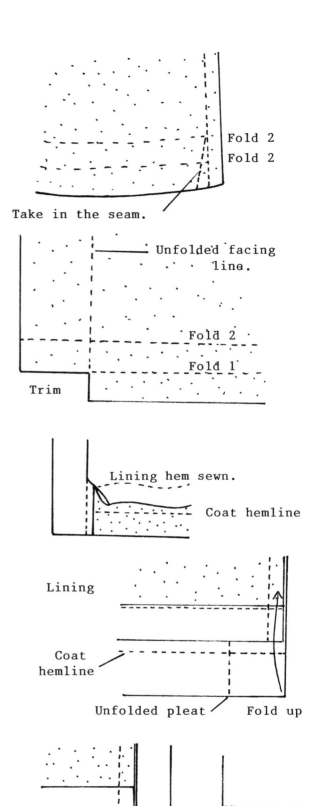

Take in the seam.

Fold 2
Fold 2

Unfolded facing line.

Fold 2
Fold 1

Trim

Lining hem sewn.

Coat hemline

Lining

Coat hemline

Unfolded pleat   Fold up

Coat hem folded up over lining hem.

Completed inside.

Shortening a Leather Coat

I will first of all caution you against doing any leather work unless you are a fairly accomplished sewer. Have leather needles and heavy duty thread and practice on leather scraps before you alter a customer's garment.

You will need to mark hems for leather coats with clothespins or clips.

The original hem will either be topstitched or glued, or both. If there is no topstitching, it has been glued and you will need to soften the glue. Do this carefully with a dry iron and press cloth. Touch the garment with the iron only long enough to warm the leather. Gently pull the old hem open, a small amount at a time.

When the hem is topstitched, remove the topstitching. If the threads are very hard to pull out, the hem is glued too. You will have to soften the glue and rip the threads, alternating each step.

Mark the new hem on the inside with chalk. Turn it up and trim off the excess. Use this for practice in topstitching so you can get the correct length and tension.

If there is no topstitching apply glue or rubber cement to the hem and coat. Allow it to become tacky and press the hem up with your hand. Hold it in place with your hand, a book, or a tailor's clapper until it is set.

Shorten the lining as needed. Refer to "Shortening Coats and Raincoats" for more details on hemming.

Lowering the Collar and Squaring the Shoulders

Lowering the Collar

Horizontal lines will form right under the collar.

Horizontal lines.

1. Pin out the excess fabric. Mark the new line.

2. If the total amount is 3/8" or less, rip the under collar and the upper collar in the area of the alteration.

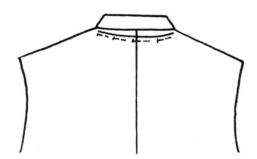

Pin out the excess.

3. Sew the upper collar to the new stitching line.

4. Trim the seam.

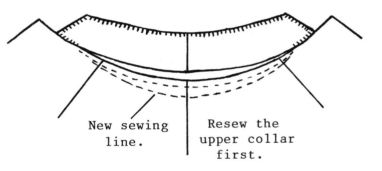

New sewing line.   Resew the upper collar first.

5. Resew the under collar by hand. Refer to the "Hand Sewing" section for details on the stitch.

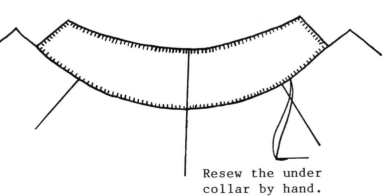

Resew the under collar by hand.

Squaring the Shoulders

If the excess fabric at the
neck is more than 3/8" total,
you must square the shoulders
too.

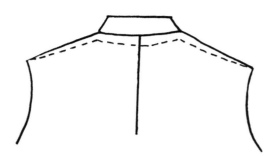

Dotted lines show new
sewing line.

1. Draw the new collar line.
You will also be taking in the
back of the shoulder seam only.

2. Rip the upper and under
collar away from the work
area.

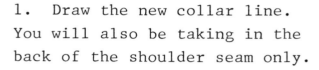

3. Rip the shoulder seam and
take in the back seam only.
The back seam will end up
being longer than the front
seam.

Rip collar and shoulder seams.

4. Trim the back seam around
the neck.

New collar
line.

5. Resew the upper collar and
then the under collar as before.

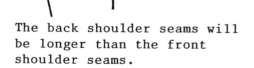

The back shoulder seams will
be longer than the front
shoulder seams.

Shortening the Collar

This alteration is needed when the coat stands away from the customer's neck in the back.

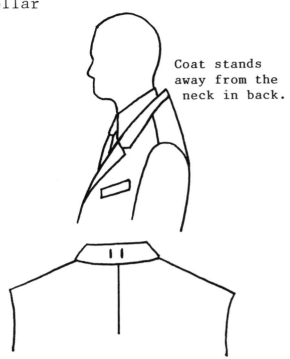

Coat stands away from the neck in back.

1. Grasp the collar of the coat at the CB and mark the extra fabric.

Mark the collar to "take in."

2. Rip the entire right side of the collar from the coat. Go to several inches past the CB seam. If there is topstitching, remove it.

*If you need to remove more than 1", do it equally from both sides.

Rip the right side of the collar from the coat.

3. Take in the CB seam the amount you marked on the collar. Make a very gradual line, tapering to nothing about 6" below the collar.

Take in the CB seam the amount you marked on the collar.

4. Rip the upper collar away from the under collar to within several inches past the CB seam.

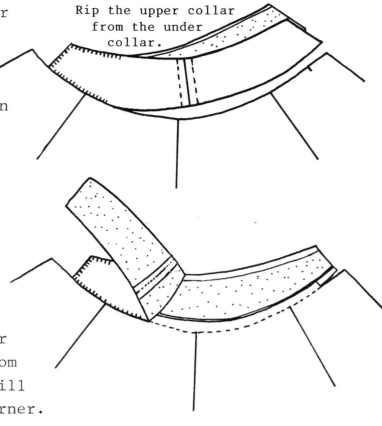

Rip the upper collar from the under collar.

5. Take in the CB seam on the under collar the same amount you took in the CB seam on the coat.

6. Resew the upper collar at the neckline, going from the CB seam out. There will be extra fabric at the corner.

Resew the upper collar to the neckline first.

7. Trim the extra fabric from the upper collar. Fold it under, sandwiching it between the under collar and the interfacing. Hand stitch it in place, checking first to see if it matches the size of the other collar corner.

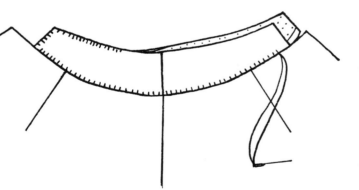

8. Replace the topstitching.

Resew the under collar by hand.

60

Shrinking the Lapels

The lapels will stand away
or "fan out" from the chest.

Lapels stand away
from the chest.

1. Shrink the lapels from
underneath by unfolding them
and easing in excess fabric.

2. Use a double thread,
waxed and knotted twice. Take
several small stitches to make
sure the thread is secure.

3. Go in and out with a small
running stitch. Alternate
pulling the thread to ease and
steaming with the iron.

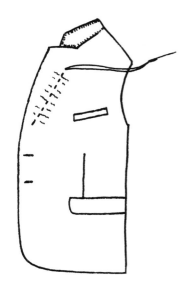

4. Secure the thread at the
top and give the lapel a soft
press. Never press a crease
on the roll line.

Refer to "Shrinking Lapels in
Vests", "Hand Sewing", and
"Pressing" for more details.

Shrink the lapels
from the underside
with needle, thread,
and steam.

Closing or Adding Vents

Once in a great while, you may be asked to add a center back vent and to close the two double back vents.

1. Pin the vents closed so they fall straight.

2. Mark the edge of the vent to show where the new sewing line will be. Take extra care when sewing the vents shut. You would be surprised at how easy it is to get bubbles and puckers in the new seams. Trim the excess from the seams.

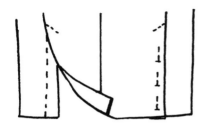

Pin the vents closed and use as guides for the new sewing lines.

3. Rip the CB seam open the length of the vent (usually about 10").

4. Use the strips you trimmed off as narrow facings for the new vent. (A narrow facing is better than no facing at all.) The left side folds over the right, so the left facing folds under and the right extends out.

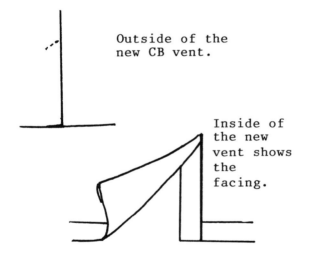

Outside of the new CB vent.

Inside of the new vent shows the facing.

5. If the coat is fully lined, rip the lining open and tack it to the vent edges by hand. If there is no lining, tack the edges of the vent to the body of the coat. You can make a small lining piece to cover the inside of the right vent.

6. Topstitch the top of the vent diagonally to reinforce it.

Interlining Coats

It is sometimes necessary in very cold climates to add interlining to overcoats.

This can be done in two ways. The first is to add a complete second lining using the original lining as a pattern. Fabric such as flannel or lightweight wool is used. The interlining is inserted between the lining and the coat.

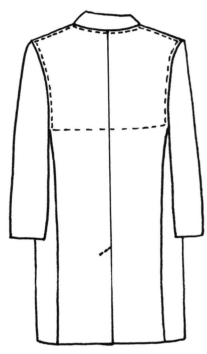

The second way is to add a partial back interlining similar to the back interfacing in jackets and coats. Draw a pattern from the coat itself and insert the interlining, tacking it to the shoulder seams, back armholes, neckline, and sides. It hangs freely at the bottom.

Dotted line shows interlining placement.

It is best to use a soft fabric, or to cut the whole piece on the bias so it will fall smoothly over the back. I have even seen a piece of chamois leather used for this purpose.

Before interlining any coat, be sure that there is enough fitting ease to allow for an added layer of fabric.

Relining Coats

The lining in coats almost always wears out before the garment itself does. So, it is not uncommon for a customer to request a new lining.

1. Rip the old lining from the coat carefully, trying not to stretch it out of shape.

Undo the collar at the neck if the lining is attached under it.

Leave the pocket welts in tact and cut the surrounding lining away.

If the welts are not worn and your new lining matches the old lining, leave the welts as is.

At the bottom of the sleeves, carefully cut the lining away from the stitching that holds the buttons on. This will save you the task of removing and resewing the lining.

2. Put markings on the sleeves to indicate where they are attached to the body to the body of the jacket.

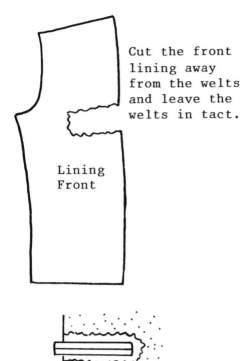

Cut the front lining away from the welts and leave the welts in tact.

Lining Front

Welts with lining cut away.

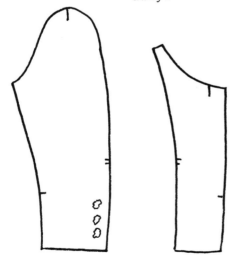

Cut lining away from buttons. Marks show connecting points.

3. Rip the lining pieces apart and press them, restoring the original shape as much as possible. Mark where they attach to each other.

4. Cut the new lining pieces. The fronts will have holes where you cut them away from the pocket welts.

Do not cut out these holes. Leave the front lining pieces whole until you sew them into the coat.

5. Sew the lining fronts to the coat facings, going as close to the pockets as possible. When you are satisfied that it is sewn in properly, slit the fabric over the welts and hand sew it to them.

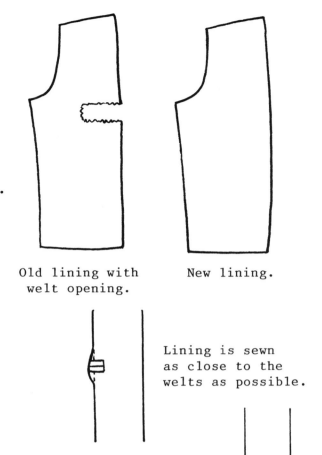

Old lining with welt opening.   New lining.

Lining is sewn as close to the welts as possible.

Slash the lining over the welts and tack down by hand.

6. Sew the CB seam and the side back seams and press.

7. Sew the shoulder seams.

8. Tack the upper collar over the back lining at the neck.

9. Tack the body of the lining to the jacket around the armholes.

10. Sew the sleeve lining in by hand as it was done originally (see "Hand Sewing"). Tack the lining to the hem and vent.

The width of lapels is determined by personal taste
and style. When lapels are
narrowed, the collar is
usually cut back the same
amount. Every jacket is
different, and if the lapels
are narrowed only slightly,
the collar may not need to
be cut back. This is mostly
up to how the area looks by
eyeballing it. Usually the
lapel notch and the collar
width are the same measurement when completed.

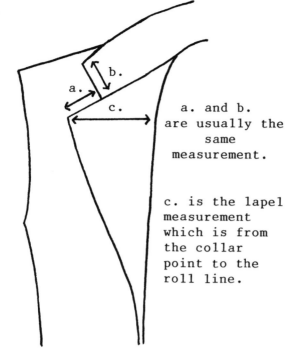

a. and b.
are usually the
same
measurement.

c. is the lapel
measurement
which is from
the collar
point to the
roll line.

1. Measure the lapel and
the collar and determine how
much each is to be narrowed.
Draw a line where the finished edges will be.

2. Go inside the jacket and
open the seam where the lining
meets the facing. Make about
a 10" opening from just above
the pocket to just below the
shoulder seam.

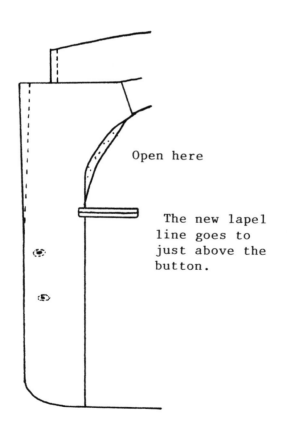

Open here

The new lapel
line goes to
just above the
button.

3. Remove the topstitching from the lapel and collar in the area where they will be narrowed.

4. Remove the collar up to the point where it will be narrowed. Cut the collar edge off ¼" from the finished line.

5. The seam that the collar was attached to will be sticking up. Clip it to the seamline at the point where the collar will end.

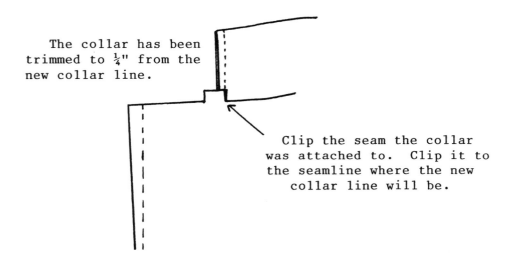

The collar has been trimmed to ¼" from the new collar line.

Clip the seam the collar was attached to. Clip it to the seamline where the new collar line will be.

6. Turn the lapel inside out through the opening in the lining. Mark your sewing line on the inside and sew the new lapel edge starting at the point where the collar stops. Sew out to the lapel point and down.

7. Trim the seam to ¼" and diagonally over the corner. Turn it right side out and press well on the under side of the lapel and collar.

8. On the under collar, cut the felt and interfacing back ¼", and fold the upper collar inside of it. Tack this together by hand. Simply put the collar back together the way it was originally. Each collar may be constructed a little differently, so no set procedure will work every time. (Refer to "Hand Sewing" chapter.)

9. Now replace the topstitching. In a very few cases, you will have to remove all the topstitching from the lapels and collar and redo it. Usually, however, the new topstitching will blend in satisfactorily where the old stopped.

10. Go back inside the jacket and handstitch the lining to the inside facing (stitch in "Hand Sewing").

11. Do a final press on the under side of the collar and lapels. This will prevent any possible scorching. If the lapels tend to stand away from the garment instead of folding back, hold the iron above them, and without touching the jacket, steam them into place. Never press a crease in the roll line because it does exactly what it says, it rolls with every movement of the body.

First press the collar and lapels on the underside.

If necessary, hold the iron above the lapels and steam them so they curve downward.

Elbow Patches

Leather elbow patches are sewn on by hand because of the difficult area in which they are located.

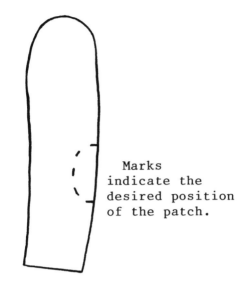

Marks indicate the desired position of the patch.

1. Put some chalk marks on one of the customer's sleeves to indicate the desired position.

2. Put the sleeve on a sleeve board, and pin the patch in place through the perforated holes.

Poorly done stitches are uneven and diagonal.

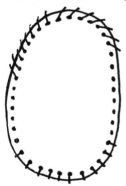

Properly done stitches are at right angles to the perforations.

3. Use a waxed double thread and sew the patch firmly to the coat. Sew right through the lining, but don't catch the cover of the board.

4. Do the other sleeve, measuring so the patches are in the same position.

Replacing a Front Jacket Zipper

When replacing a jacket zipper, always do one side first and then the other. If the fabric is not the type that can be pinned (such as in skiwear), sew the zipper to the outer fabric first. Then hold the lining in place and topstitch from the front of the outer fabric. Make sure the jacket is perfectly even at the top and bottom. Place a small row of zig-zag at the bottom of the zipper for durability.

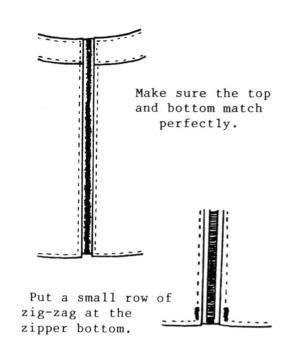

Make sure the top and bottom match perfectly.

Put a small row of zig-zag at the zipper bottom.

Replacing a Ski Jacket Pocket Zipper

Go to the inside of the jacket by ripping the coat from the lining at the front zipper or hem just below the pocket. Remove the back of the pocket so the zipper is exposed. Rip the zipper out. Replace the zipper by topstitching it in place from the jacket front. Resew the back of the pocket and the lining to the coat.

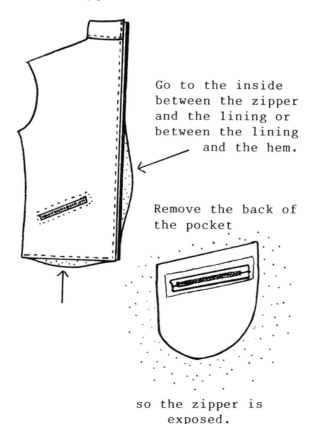

Go to the inside between the zipper and the lining or between the lining and the hem.

Remove the back of the pocket

so the zipper is exposed.

70

Shirt Alterations

Shortening the Sleeves

1. Pin a fold of fabric around the sleeve above the placket.

2. Measure the amount of the fold. Remove the pins and transfer the marks to the bottom of the sleeve.

3. Remove the cuff, pinning pleats above the alteration line if there are any.

4. If the sleeves are shortened more than 1", remove the placket and move it up. Do one side at a time so you can have the other side for a guide.

5. Trim fabric at the bottom to 5/8" from the new seamline.

6. Reapply the cuff on the new sewing line and topstitch if needed.

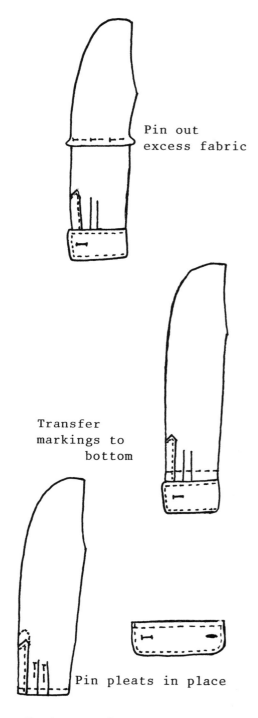

Pin out excess fabric

Transfer markings to bottom

Pin pleats in place

Move placket up if needed

Making Short Sleeves

Short sleeves are usually
9" from the shoulder seam.
When the customer has a
shirt he likes, always take
the measurement from it.

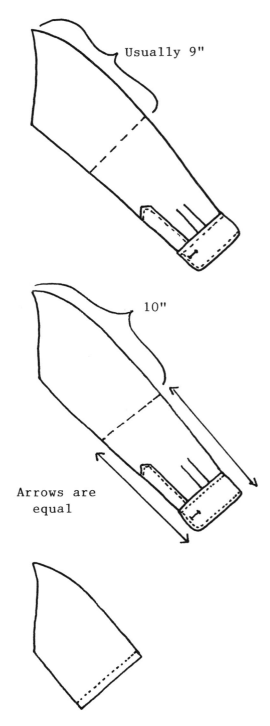

Usually 9"

1. Measure down from the
shoulder seam 10" (9" + 1"
for the hem). Make a mark.

10"

2. Measure from the bottom
of the sleeve up. Go to the
underarm seam of the sleeve
and measure from the bottom
up the same distance. Put
a mark and connect them with
a line.

Arrows are
equal

3. Cut the sleeve off.

4. Turn the hem under ½"
and ½" again. Stitch and
press the new hem.

Finished sleeve

73

Shortening the Shirt

For a shirt with a straight bottom, measure the amount to be shortened and redo the hem, duplicating the original hem as closely as possible. If it is a narrow rolled hem, try to make use of the machine attachment that does this.

When shortening any shirt, take into consideration the position of the bottom button and buttonhole. The shirt may have to be slightly longer or shorter than marked, if the buttonhole falls right on the desired hemline.

A curved bottom is done just like a straight bottomed hem with one exception. If there is a very large curve up to the sides, don't shorten the sides as much as the front and back, or they may come above the waist.

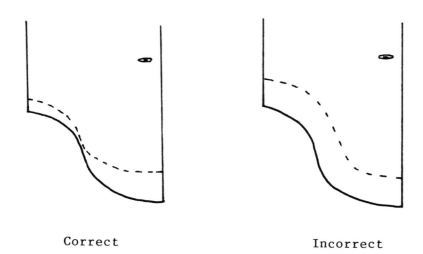

Correct   Incorrect

Adding Back Darts

Darts may be added in the back of the shirt to take out some fullness.

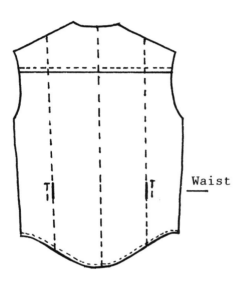

1. Picture three imaginary lines down the back of the shirt, dividing it into four equal parts. One line goes through the CB and the other two lines divide the sides of the back equally.

2. Determine where the waist is and take two folds of fabric on the side back lines. These will be the widest points of the darts.

3. Pin up to nothing at the bottom of the shoulder blades and down to nothing about 2" from the shirt bottom (or pin all the way through the hem if needed).

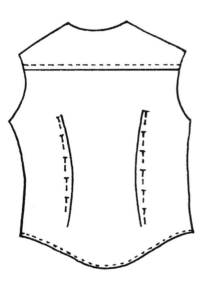

4. Transfer the marks to the inside, connect them with chalk, and sew. Press toward the CB.

Darts pinned on outside

Taking in the Sideseams

If the customer wants the sides taken in, always check to see if the seams are flat felled (double top-stitched) because this will add a lot of time onto the length of the alteration. If the seams are flat felled, check first to see if back darts will remove enough fullness. If not, be sure to give a price quote which reflects the extra time that will be needed to do the alteration.

1. Pin the sides as needed.

2. If you are extending the alteration into the armhole, taper it to nothing as soon as possible.

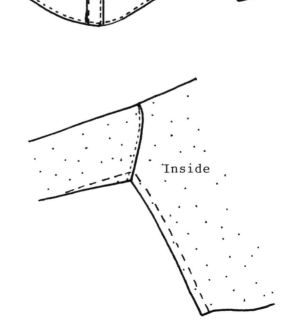

If the seams are flat felled, remove all the stitching first and then sew the new seam.

3. Transfer markings to the inside and sew the new seams.

4. Trim and finish the seams.

Inside

Narrowing the Collar

More appropriate terms for narrowing the collar might be restyling or reshaping because it is done in order to update the lines.

To determine the new collar lines, copy a collar the customer likes, or pin the collar under to obtain the desired shape. This is done in the area of the collar points only. The back of the collar is not narrowed, nor is the length of the collar shortened at the neckline.

Dots show new collar lines

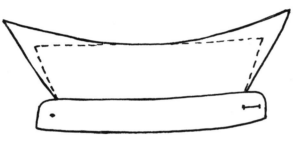

1. Remove the collar and rip out the topstitching if there is any. If the collar is on a neck band, remove the collar but leave the band in place. If there are collar stays, remove them permanently.

2. Turn the collar inside out and transfer the markings to the inside. It may help to press the seams and collar flat before you sew.

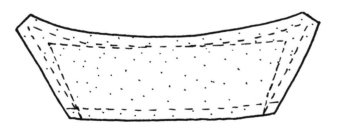

Collar turned inside out

3. When sewing the new lines, stitch from the CB out and down. Turn the collar and stitch from the CB out and down the other way. This will help keep the collar symmetrical.

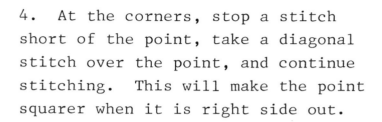

Sew from center out and down, taking one or two diagonal stitches at the corners.

4. At the corners, stop a stitch short of the point, take a diagonal stitch over the point, and continue stitching. This will make the point squarer when it is right side out.

5. Trim the seams closely. Trim diagonally over the points.

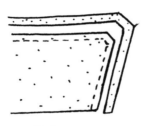

Trim

6. After trimming, turn the collar right side out and press. Replace the topstitching, stretching the edges of the collar slightly as you go. To keep the points of the collar from being "eaten" by the machine, thread a needle and take a stitch through the point. Pull on the thread when you sew around the point.

Threaded needle keeps corners from being "eaten" by the machine.

7. Resew the collar to the shirt or to the neck band.

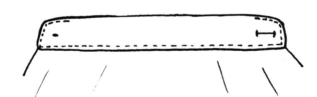

Resew collar to neck band.

78

Adding Collar Buttons and Buttonholes

1. Have the customer put the shirt on with a tie. Put a pin in each side of the shirt to mark where the buttons should go. It is very hard to determine this if you don't do it on the customer.

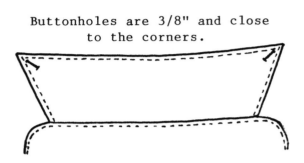

Buttonholes are 3/8" and close to the corners.

2. Collar buttons are usually ¼" and the buttonholes are 3/8" because of all the thicknesses of fabric they are in.

Position them diagonally at the collar points, as close to the topstitching as possible.

3. In order to keep your machine from "eating" the collar points, sew a piece of non-fusible interfacing to the underside of the collar. Attach it by stitching right over the topstitching at the corners of the collar.

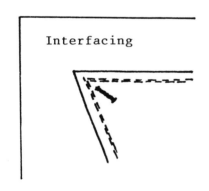

Interfacing

4. When the machine is making the buttonhole, hold the interfacing taut. Afterwards, rip the stitching and cut the interfacing away.

5. Slash the buttonhole and sew on the button. Give it a strong shank.

Sewing on Emblems

When sewing emblems on the upper arm of shirt sleeves, press them in half and then position them on the sleeve crease. Be sure to ask the customer how far down from the shoulder he wants the emblem. I recommend hand basting or pinning to hold it in place for sewing. If you glue or fuse them on first, it may be hard to correct an error later.

If you have to sew an emblem on a shirt pocket, rip off half the pocket, sew on the emblem, and resew the pocket. If you cannot match the stitching, remove the entire pocket first.

Sew all emblems on with a small, straight stitch, not a zig-zag. Always try to match the thread and sew where it won't show, as close to the edge as possible.

Monogramming

I would advise that unless you are an expert monogrammer or have a monogramming machine, that you do not risk tackling this job. I have found that a regular sewing machine is very hard to adjust for monogramming and the process is time-consuming. The problem is magnified because men usually don't want a shirt monogrammed unless it has been custom made or is very expensive. This makes it much harder for you to replace if you ruin it.

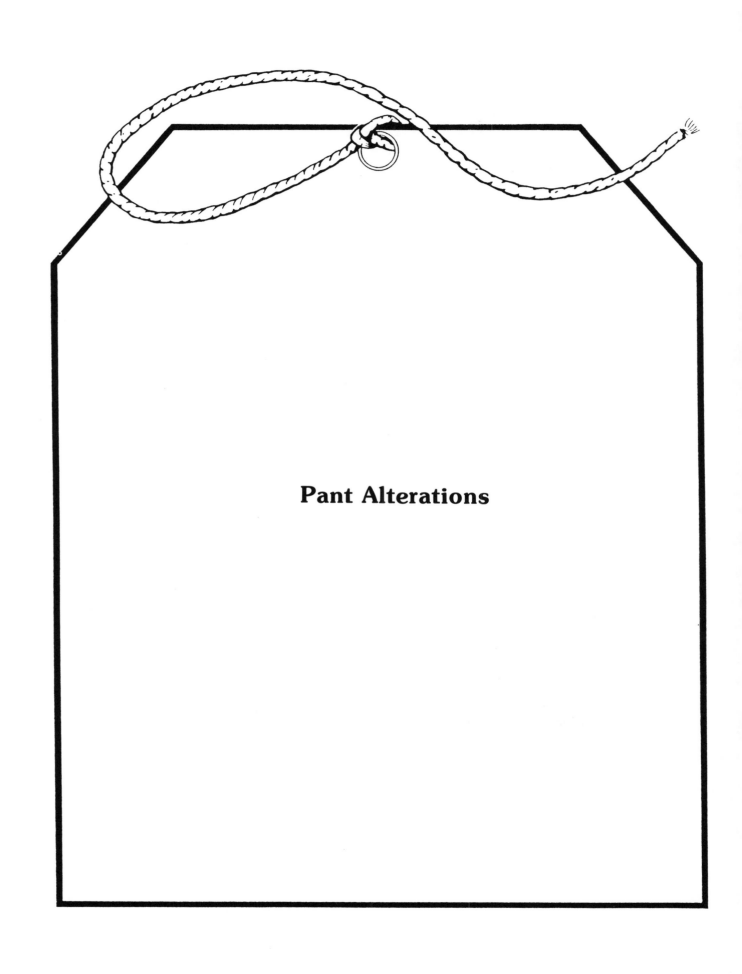

Pant Alterations

The length of the pants will be up to the customer's personal preference. Ask him if he wants the hem to just touch the top of the shoe or if he wants a break. The majority of customers will want a break.

Also ask if he wants plain bottoms or cuffs. Many men still wear cuffs and you will need to ask the size.

I recommend pinning the hem so the customer can see the results. Always pin or mark both legs. Everyone has a slight difference in the length of their legs, and some can vary as much as 1½". After pinning, reinforce the marks with chalk so they won't be lost if the pins fall out.

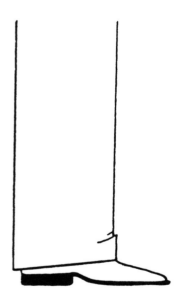

Slight break in the front, tapered down in the back.

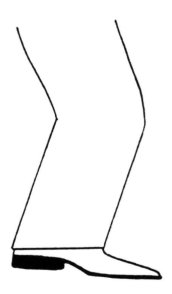

When the knee is bent, the break vanishes.

Plain Bottomed Hem

1. Remove the old hem.

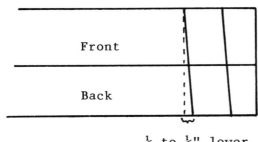

2. Lay the pants out flat and draw a chalk line from the front chalk mark to the back chalk mark.

¼ to ½" lower

Be sure that the back mark is at least ¼" lower than the front mark. This causes what is called a "tip" on the hem and makes the hem more pleasing to the eye.

At times a customer will request a larger tip, in which case you would follow his instructions.

3. Measure the hem length and cut off the excess. Commercial hems are usually 1¼ to 1½". This is done to save fabric. I recommend using 2¼ to 2½" as your hem length and the pant will fall better.

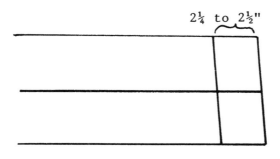

2¼ to 2½"

4. Finish the raw edge by serging it. If you do not have a serger, cut it with a pinking shears.

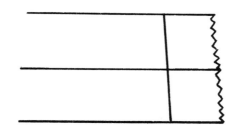

5. Fold the hem under and press it. Some men will request a heel guard. This is a piece of dark twill tape about ½" wide. It is sewn to the inside bottom of the hem to prevent wear. Sew it in at this time.

6. Sew the hem using a blindhemmer or refer to the hand stitch directions in the "Hand Sewing" section.

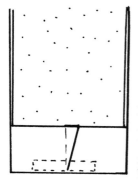

Dotted line shows where the heel guard would be located.

Tuck in CB hem

7. Depending on the amount of tip, the turned-up hem may not seem to fit the pant. It will be too tight in the front and too large in the back if the tip is over ¼".

Allow the hem to lie flat by taking a tuck in the center of the back hem and by opening the sideseams slightly to make extra ease for the front. Take a few tiny hand stitches to tack down the partially opened sideseams.

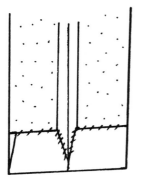

Back   Front

Opened sideseam

8. Press the finished hem.

84

Cuffs

1. Mark the hem front and back and ask the customer what width cuff he wants (1¼" is the average). Be sure to see if there is enough fabric. You will need 3 times the cuff width. For a 1¼" cuff, that would be 3 3/4" past the hemline.

2. Draw the hemline. It will be very difficult to have the cuff lie smoothly with more than ½" tip. A ¼" tip is really ideal.

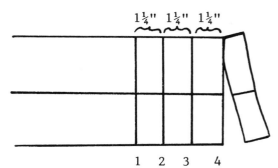

3. Draw 3 more lines the width of the cuff.

4. Cut off on the last line. Turn the raw edge under ¼" and press or stitch to hold it. If the fabric is very bulky, cut the ¼" off with pinking shears or finish after cutting.

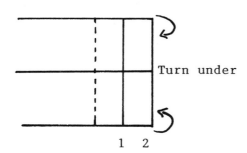

Turn under

5. Fold the hem under at the second line and stitch through the ¼" turnunder.

6. Fold the cuff up on the hemline and press.

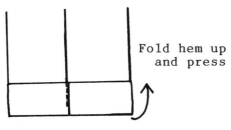

Fold hem up and press

Stitch the ditch at the sideseam

7. Tack the cuff in place by stitching the ditch in the sideseam and inseam.

Levi Hems

Sewing levi hems is always traumatic because of snapping needles and because of the difficulty in trying to match topstitching thread.

Change to a heavy duty needle or try a leather needle. I usually expect to break at least one needle sewing a denim hem so I charge a little extra for levis.

After marking, rolling up the hem, and pressing, try giving the thick folds of fabric at the seams a few hits with a hammer. Be sure to have a solid surface underneath.

If you cannot find heavy duty thread to match, try using two threads in the top and one bobbin thread. If you do this, you will have to sew on the outside of the garment so the double thread will be outside where you want it to show.

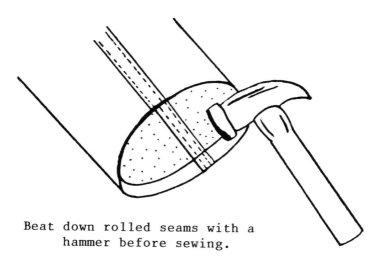

Beat down rolled seams with a
hammer before sewing.

Lengthening

Lengthening pants poses two problems. First, there may not be enough fabric to leave a wide enough hem. In this case, you will use purchased hem tape for a facing or you can make your own. If you make your own, it will be much easier to work with if you cut it on the bias. The most important thing to remember is not to stretch the facing while you're sewing it on. After you have applied it, press it. Then press the hem up and proceed as for a normal hem.

The second problem you may have to deal with is that the old hemline may show. If the line is not soiled, squirt water directly on it and press with a cloth. On light colors, you can also try putting diluted white vinegar on the crease and pressing. I am generally unsuccessful at using spot removers when the line is discolored because the stain is usually well set. I find that if the customer is willing, topsitiching over the old hemline is a good disguise. This, of course, is only appropriate with sportswear.

Pants with Zippers in the Hemline

With the physical fitness craze have come sweatpants with zippers at the hem. If the pants need to be shortened more than 1½", you should move the zipper up the same amount the pants are being shortened. Otherwise, you will probably be able to cut the zipper off at the bottom. Just remember to fold the ends under and topstitch several times since you will be cutting off the zipper stop.

Taking In

1. Grasp the excess fabric
at the waist and mark it on
each side with chalk. You
may want to secure it with a
pin so you can continue
chalking into the seat area.

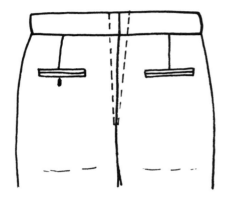

2. Go to the inside and rip
the stitching that is holding
the waistband down. It may
be held down only by the
stitching from the belt loop
if there is one.

Chalk marks show where
the waist and seat are
to be taken in.

3. Transfer the markings to the inside and connect
them to form a good curve. It is very important to
draw a smooth CB seam and seat curve. This is necessary to get a good fit and in order to avoid puckers
on the outside of the seam. You may have to deviate
slightly from your markings to form this line properly.
There is no set curve formation, but with experience
you will learn to draw one that works.

Inside markings

Poorly drawn
line

Good line

4. Sew the new line twice for extra strength. Sew from the top down.

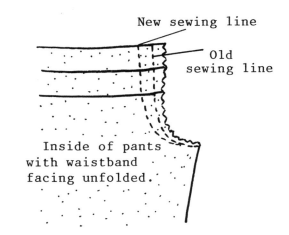

New sewing line

Old sewing line

Inside of pants with waistband facing unfolded.

5. Rip the old stitching and trim the seam if it is over 1½". It is best to serge the raw edge, but if you can't, trim it with a pinking shears.

* Sometimes only the seat needs to be taken in. Here, again, it is important to get a good curve.

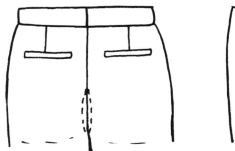

Marks for taking in the seat.

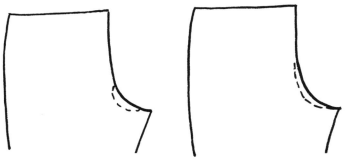

Poorly drawn curve.

Smooth curve.

6. Press the seam open.

7. Fold the waistband facing down and press. Secure it by stitching the ditch on the outside where the waistband joins the pant. Resew the belt loop if there was one.

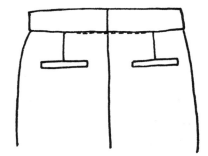

Letting Out

1. Before the customer tries the pants on, measure how much there is to let out. I prefer to then have the customer put them on. Ask him to unbutton the pants in front and unzip them slightly. Measure the amount of gap. I do this so I can see how far down in the seat they need to be let out. If you are un-comfortable doing this, just measure his waist and let the pants out that much, tapering to nothing in the seat.

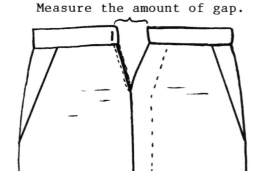

Measure the amount of gap.

2. Sew the new seam twice.

3. Rip out the old stitching being very careful not to cut the fabric.

4. Press the seam open and secure the waistband. Warn the customer in advance that the old seam may show slightly if the pants aren't new.

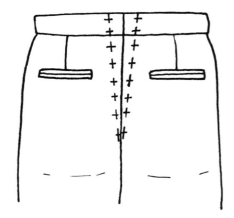

Markings mean "let the waist and seat out this much."

Waist, Seat, and Stride

Taking In

It is common when taking in the waist and seat, to also take in the stride. This corrects the bagginess in the back of the thighs.

1. If the waist is too big, first put a pin in it to hold it in place.

2. Next pinch a horizontal fold of fabric out of the CB seam. Pinch enough so the seam does not hang loosely on the seat anymore.

3. Make two chalk marks to signify the width of the pinch and remove the pin.

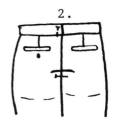

4. Now pin all the way from the waist through the seat as far as is needed. Disregard bagginess in the thighs. (If the customer has lost 35 pounds or more, the pants probably cannot be altered.)

5. Taking in the stride is another way of saying that you are removing bagginess from the back of the thighs. Go back to the pinch you took out of the CB seam and measure it. This will be the amount to be removed from the stride.

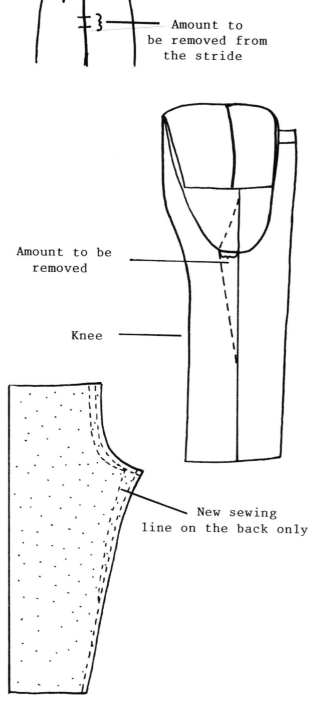

Amount to be removed from the stride

Amount to be removed

Knee

New sewing line on the back only

6. On the outside of the pants back, start at the bottom of the crotch line starting with the stride measurement. Taper to nothing just below the knee.

7. Rip the lower crotch seam and the leg seam and remove the amount marked from the back pant leg only. This removes the extra fabric from the back of the thigh. If you remove more than 1½", trim some of the seam allowance, but leave at least 1".

8. Next, take in the waist and seat as described earlier.

9. Taking in the stride will cause the back crease to move inward. Lay the pants out and press in a new back crease from just below the knee up.

Letting Out

There has usually been a large seam allowed in the stride of men's pants, so you will be able to let it out.

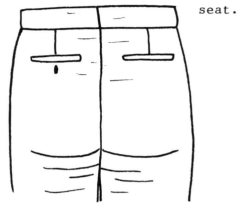

Pull lines at waist and tight seat.

The pants will be pulling at the back of the thighs.

Again, it is hard to determine how much to let out
the stride because there is
no way to measure this. I
usually let the amount of
increase in the waist and
seat determine how much I
let out the stride.

Pull lines at back of thighs.

In general, if the pants
are let out in the waist
and seat 1" to 1½", I would
let out the stride about 1".
This is only on the back seam.
If the waist and seat were
let out more than 1½" and the
stride looked very tight, I
would let it out about 1 3/4
to 2".

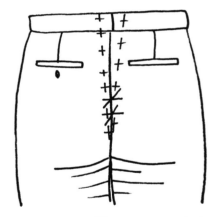

Marks mean "let out waist,
seat, and stride."

If there is not enough fabric to let out in the back
seam, you may be able to add a crotchpiece (refer to
the "Crotch Adjustment" section for details on this).

Crotch Adjustment

Taking in the Crotch

1. If the crotch needs to be taken in, the customer will usually complain that he feels the pants "bubble out" or that there is extra fabric in the crotch area.

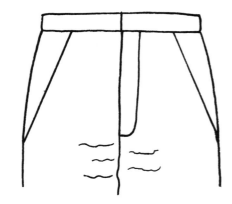

Fabric bubbles in front

This is different from the crotch depth being too long, which is corrected by dropping the waistband.

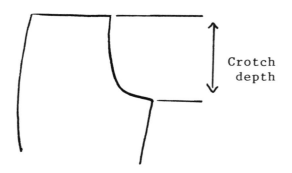

Crotch depth

Extra crotch fabric usually occurs because the crotch curve is too long.

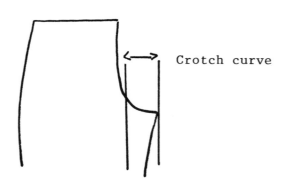

Crotch curve

2. Fabric will need to be pinned out of the front seams only just below the crotch. If you are uncomfortable doing this or if you feel the customer will be embarrassed, make a mental estimate of the amount to be taken in.

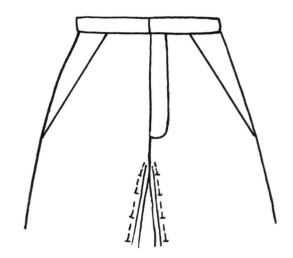

Fabric pinned out of front only

Ask the customer to remove the pants so you can pin them. Then he can slip them on again to check the fit.

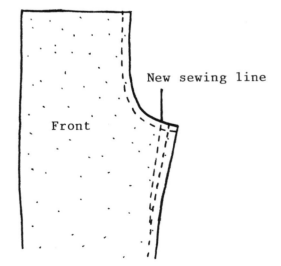

New sewing line

Front

3. Draw your new lines and take in on the front seam only.

Letting Out the Crotch

1. When the crotch needs
to be let out, the customer
will almost always state
that the pants feel too tight
in the crotch. The pants will
have pull lines comming directly from the crotch.

Pull lines at crotch

2. Since it is hard to fit
this problem, you will get
an idea of how much to let
out by asking the customer
if the crotch is slightly
tight or very tight.

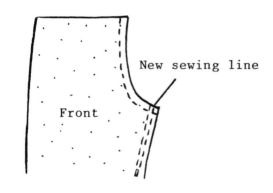

New sewing line

Front

If he replies, "Just a little tight," it probably needs
to be let out ¼ to ½".

Depending upon how much fabric there is in the seam,
you may have to let out the
back seam too, especially if
the customer says the crotch
is very tight. Let the seams
out, tapering to nothing about
4" below the crotch. Sew
these new seams twice since the
crotch is a high stress area.

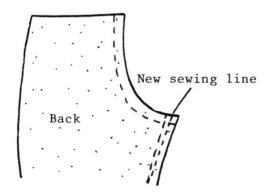

New sewing line

Back

96

Adding a Crotchpiece

If the customer has gained
weight, wants extra fabric
in the crotch for ease of
movement (such as in sportswear), or has a worn area in
the crotch, you can some-
times add a crotchpiece.
The crotchpiece is a trian-
gular piece of fabric, usually about 6" long, and as
wide at the top as is needed.

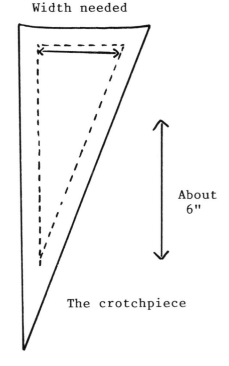

Width needed

About
6"

The crotchpiece

Of course, a crotchpiece
can only be added if there
is matching fabric avail-
able. Sometimes a piece
can be taken from the hem.

The crotchpiece is
added at the inseam.

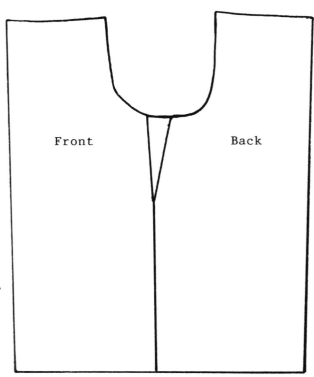

Front   Back

Reshaping the Crotch

The customer's pants could fit well all over, but
he may complain that he can, "feel them in the seat."
This usually means that the lower seat curve is not
coinciding with the shape of his body. This will be
in the lower seat area.

After you have determined that there are no other
problems with the pants, note on the ticket, "Reshape
binding seat," or, "Reshape seat curve." Put one
chalk mark across the seam at the location of the problem.

Go to the inside and redraw the crotch curve. You
will be amazed at how ¼ to ½" difference in the curve
can change the feel of the pants.

Do not change it more than ¼" for the first try.
As you sew, stretch the seam. Trim the seam following
your new curve.

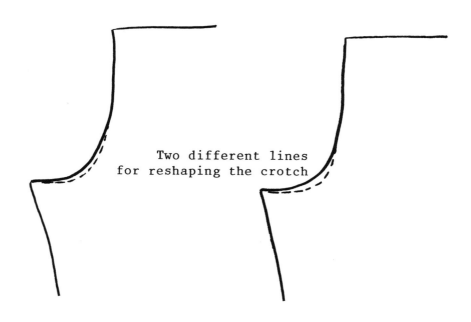

Two different lines
for reshaping the crotch

Lining the Crotch

1. If you are asked to line the crotch, go to the inside and trace a pattern from the pants.

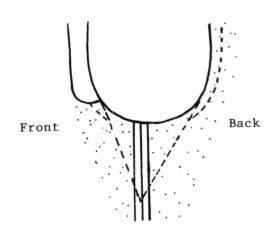

Front   Back

Trace a pattern

Start at the bottom of the fly and follow the curved crotch about 3" into the seat. Go down 4" into the inseam.

2. Cut the pattern 4 times so you will have 2, two-sided linings. Add 3/8" to each straight side for seam allowance.

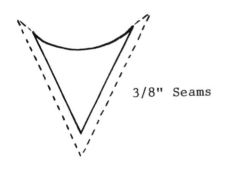

3/8" Seams

3. Sew the straight sides leaving the curved edges open.

4. Turn and press.
5. Pink or serge the curved edges.
6. Sew the lining right into the crotch seam.
7. Tack it to the inseam by hand underneath.

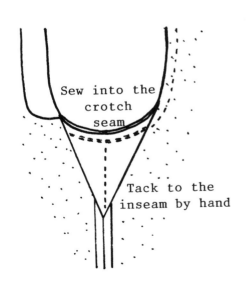

Sew into the crotch seam

Tack to the inseam by hand

Taking In

Men's sideseams are very rarely taken in. This
is because men do not carry a lot of weight on their
hips, and when they lose weight, it doesn't usually
affect the sideseams. Taking in the sideseams is also
avoided because of the pockets.

If the pockets are like either of the two types
below, ¼ to ½" could be removed without redoing them.

The sideseams can
be taken up to the
dotted lines.

If you need to take in the sideseams more than ½",
or if the pockets are like the ones below, you must remove the pockets and facings, and move them in. Do one
side first and use the other as a guide.

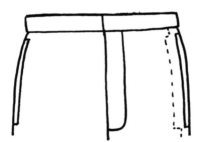

Dotted lines show
new pocket location.

Letting Out

Sideseams usually cannot be let out because of the
pockets. In rare cases, the back sideseams only can be
let out.

Dropping the Waistband

This alteration is needed when the rise (equivalent to the crotch depth in women's clothing) is too low. The pants will basically fit well but will hang down in the crotch. The waistband cannot be dropped more than 1" or the fly and pockets will be too short.

1. Pin or chalk out the ridge of extra fabric just under the waistband.

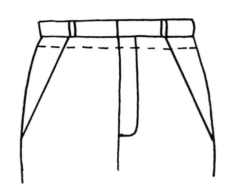

2. Measure the amount folded out and mark the new sewing line on the pants.

Marks for dropping the waistband

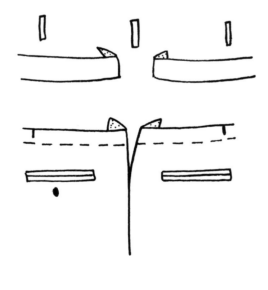

3. Remove the waistband, being sure to mark where it was attached at the CF, CB, and sideseams. Also mark belt loop locations. The waistband will be in two pieces because men's have a seam in the CB. You will have to rip down a few inches into the CB seam.

If there is a small pocket
in the waist seam, you will
have to move it down. It
may simply be a slit, or it
may have a flap too. Note
how the pocket is made and
move it down to the new
seamline.

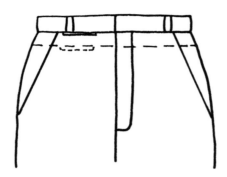

Plain watch pocket

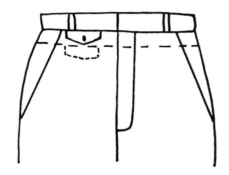

Watch pocket with a flap

If the pants have belt loops
that were sewn into the seam,
baste them in place. Basting
will help you avoid sewing
over pins, and you will not
lose a belt loop if a pin
falls out.

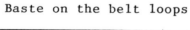

Baste on the belt loops

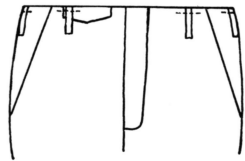

You may also have to move
the fly facing down if the
button tab will be too high
after the waistband is
dropped. Remove the whole
facing piece and move it
down the amount you are
dropping the waistband.
You may need to shorten
it at the bottom.

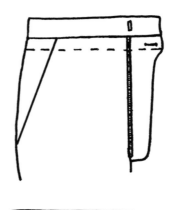

4. Resew the waistband,
easing in the pant waist.

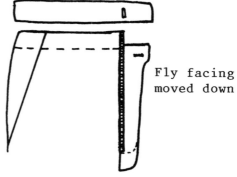

Fly facing
moved down

5. The seam is usually
pressed open.

6. Resew the CB seam.

7. You may want to stitch
the ditch all around the
waistband.

8. Sew down the belt loops.

Stitch the ditch at the waist

103

Tapering Pant Legs

This alteration is done to update out-of-style pants, or to scale down pant legs so they are more in proportion with the customer's body. Take the measurement from a pair of pants the customer likes, because it is too hard to judge the width by pinning on the body.

1. Measure across the very bottom of the pant leg to determine the old and new widths.

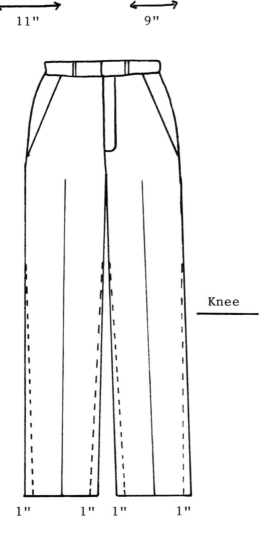

2. Subtract the desired width from the old width. In this case it would be 11" - 9" = 2".

3. Divide this amount by 2 and remove that much from each sideseam: 2" ÷ 2" = 1".

4. Remove the hem and draw the new sewing line, tapering to nothing about 3" above the knee.

5. Rip out the old seamline and trim the seams. Press the seams open.

6. Resew the hem and press. The pant creases remain the same.

Swinging the Creases

This alteration is necessary when the creases do not hang straight down the center of the leg. It is not uncommon to have only one crooked crease. This happens for any one of several reasons, including having bowed legs, being pigeon-toed or knock-kneed, or from having a high hip. The creases may turn inward or outward.

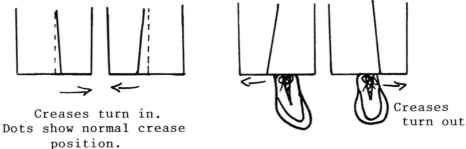

Creases turn in.
Dots show normal crease position.

Creases turn out

Measure for this by putting a chalk mark on the pant hem at the middle of the shoe. This is where you want the crease to fall. Mark each leg because the amounts may be different, or you may be changing only one leg. The distance from the chalk mark to the crease is the amount you will swing the crease.

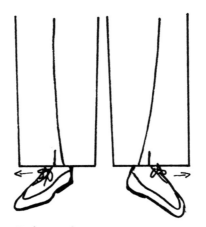

Swing these creases out.

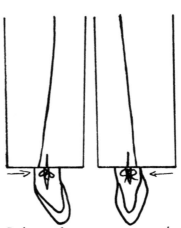

Swing these creases in.

Swinging the Creases Inward

1. Put a chalk mark on the front inseam about 3" below the knee.

2. Measure the amount the crease needs to be swung, and put a chalk mark that distance on the back inseam. Put it below the front mark.

3. On the outseam, put a chalk mark on the front about 3" below the knee.

4. On the back outseam, put a mark the amount to swung, above the other mark.

5. Remove the hem.

6. Rip the inseam and outseam open to about 4" above the knee.

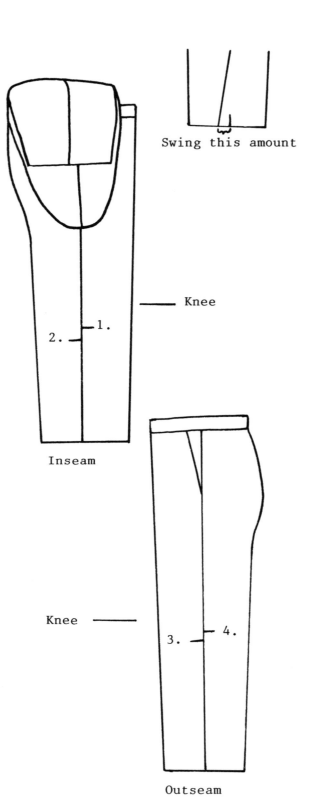

Swing this amount

Knee

2. ⌐1.

Inseam

Knee

3. ⌐ 4.

Outseam

7. On the inseam you will be moving the front down and the back will be eased up. This will pull the crease inward. The bottom edge will be uneven and the two marks should come close to matching.

8. Do the same procedure on the outseam. In this case, the front will be eased up and the back will come down.

9. Press the seams well and try not to let any of the easing show.

10. Lay the pants out and redraw the hemline. Using the front and back creases as your guides. The pant bottom will be uneven. Resew the hem.

11. Do the same procedure on the other leg if needed.

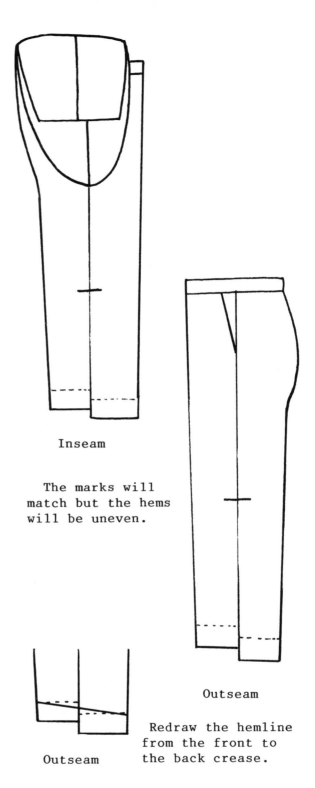

Inseam

The marks will match but the hems will be uneven.

Outseam

Redraw the hemline from the front to the back crease.

Outseam

Swinging Creases Outward

Follow all the steps for "Swinging Creases Inward",
but reverse the directions of the marks.

Below I have made a master chart to aid you in
sewing and marking. *Caution: do not try to simply
press a new crease in order to solve the problem. If
you do, the new crease won't be on the grain and it
will never hold.

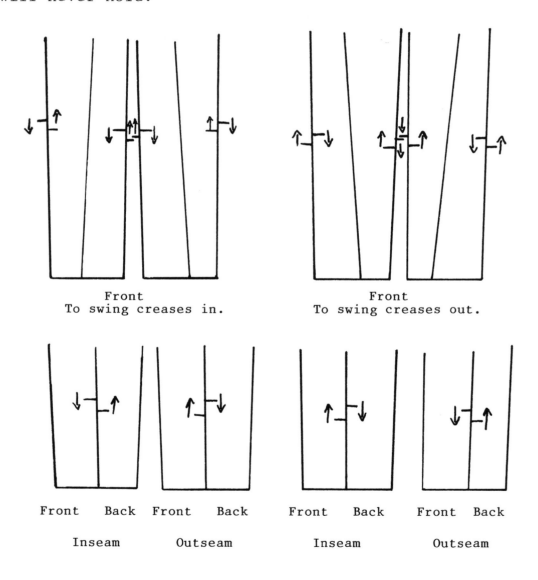

Front
To swing creases in.

Front
To swing creases out.

Front	Back	Front	Back	Front	Back	Front	Back
Inseam		Outseam		Inseam		Outseam	

108

Lining

Men's pants are usually lined only to the knee and only in the front. This is needed when the customer is sensitive to wool or to something else in the fabric that makes him itch.

It is easier to buy a pants pattern in the size and style of the customer's pants than to try to draw a pattern yourself. Measure the waist, hips, crotch depth, and pant front, and compare the measurements to the pattern. Adjust it accordingly.

I cut 1" instead of 5/8" seams so I will have extra fabric if needed.

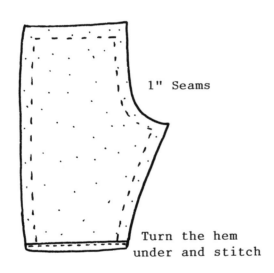

1" Seams

Turn the hem under and stitch

1. Finish the edge at the bottom with serging or turn it under twice and stitch. Serge all the edges or trim them with a pinking shears.

2. Sew the inseam side right into the pant seam. Sew up to the crotch as closely as you can go.

Lining is sewn to the inseam of the pants

3. Clip the crotch seam and pin it under. Continue to turn it under and pin it to the edge of the fly facing and up to the waist.

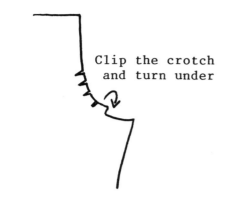

Clip the crotch and turn under

4. Undo the stitching that is holding the waistband facing down and extend the lining up under it.

5. Pin the lining to the outseam, turning it under as needed to fit.

6. Stitch the lining to the crotch seam and outseam by hand.

7. Stitch the ditch of the waistband to secure the lining there. Stitch from the outside.

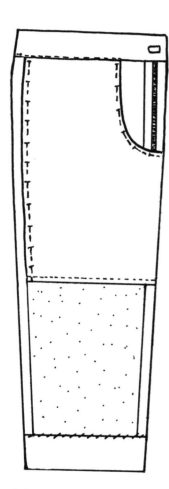

Inside of pant showing lining

110

Replacing the Zipper

1. Rip out the old zipper, carefully marking the sewing lines. You will also have to rip out part of the waistband that encloses the top ends of the zipper.

2. Rip out the topstitching from the fly, marking the line if it is not visible.

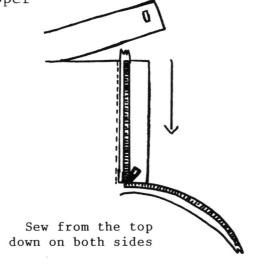

Sew from the top down on both sides

3. As you look at the pants, stitch the left side of the zipper from the top down. You may have to stop and move the zipper pull up or down as you go to get it out of the way.

4. Restitch the waistband.

5. Unfold the fly and pin or baste the other side of the zipper to it. Sew from the top down. The zipper will be face down.

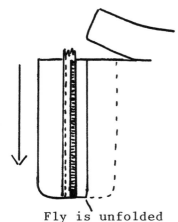

Fly is unfolded

6. Resew the topstitching from the bottom up, trying not to catch the facing from the right side. Put the facing in its original position and bar tack through all the layers.

7. Resew the waistband.

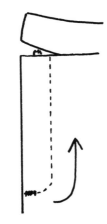

Replace topstitching from the bottom up

Belt Loops

Applying Premade Belt Loops

1. Ask the customer what width belt he wears.

2. Cut loops the width of the belt plus 1". The 1" allows for 3/8" seams and ¼" extra for ease over the belt.

3. You will need a minimum of 5 loops, 7 are preferred.

4. Undo the waistband facing all around.

5. Rip open a small part of the waist seam and insert the belt loops at the intervals pictured below. Go to the inside and stitch it into the seam, using a 3/8" seam on the belt loops. The loop at CB will not be inserted into the seam, but topstitched in place. If you only have 5 loops, omit the ones over the back pockets, and move the ones over the sideseams toward the back about an inch.

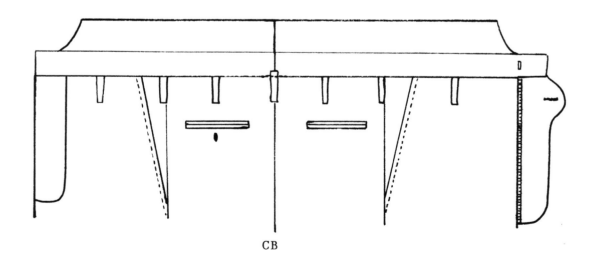

CB

Belt loop placement

6. If the loops are ¼" or more wider than the waist-band, remembering to leave a 3/8" seam at the top, stitch them down to the front of the pant.

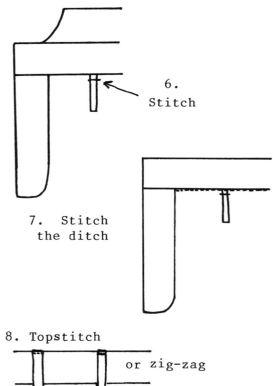

6. Stitch

7. Stitch the ditch

8. Topstitch   or zig-zag

7. Fold the facing down and stitch the ditch.

8. Fold the belt loop up. Turn 3/8" under and stitch across several times, or use a small zig-zag.

Making New Belt Loops

Fabric is usually taken from the hem to make new belt loops. Even if you don't use it all, remove the same amount from each hem so they won't be uneven. You may have to face the hems.

Belt loops are 3/8" wide so you will need a minimum of 1". This only leaves 1/8" seams, so it is desirable to have a wider strip if possible.

Sew the strip and turn it right side out. Follow the previous directions for applying them.

Make one long strip and cut into the desired lengths

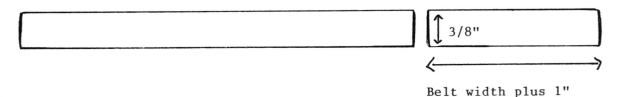

3/8"

Belt width plus 1"

Pockets

Half Pocket

It is not uncommon for front pants
pockets to wear through. If the
damage is only in the bottom, you
can make a new half pocket.

1. Cut off the damaged area and
use it for a pattern.

2. Rip the stitching and unfold
the pocket. Cut a new piece adding
1" on the top seam for seam allowances.

*Try to purchase pocketing fabric
at a tailor supply store because it
is very durable. If you cannot,
duplicate the fabric as closely as
possible.

3. Stitch the inside of the pocket
pieces together. This will put the
seam on the outside of the pocket.
Use a ½" seam.

4. Press the seam allowances down.
Turn them under and topstitch.

5. Fold the pocket so the outsides
are together. Bring the pocket inside out to the right side of the
pants so you can sew the seam.

6. Pull the pocket back to the inside and topstitch the bottom.

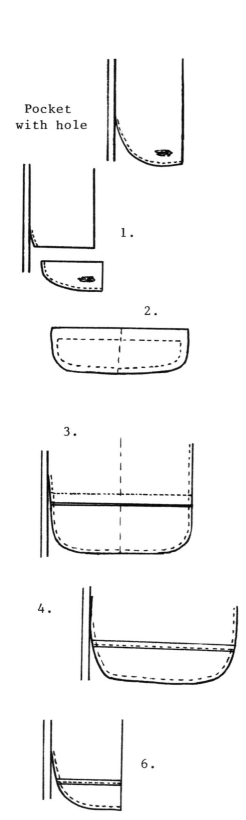

Pocket
with hole

1.

2.

3.

4.

6.

114

Full Pocket

If the pocket is worn in the upper half, or if the customer insists on replacing the whole pocket, you will have to do so.

There are many different ways that pockets are constructed, so do one side at a time and use the other for a guide.

The first time you do this, it will seem impossible. Take your time and you will succeed. Be sure to rip enough of the waistband facing out of your way so you can get to the top of the pocket easily.

Because this is very time-consuming, give a price quote first. Depending on the quality of the pants, the customer may ask you to just mend the hole as best you can.

Watch Pocket

This is a small pocket inserted in the right front waist seam. Discuss with the customer the width of the opening. You will be limited by the small area in which you will be working. A watch pocket is usually 2½ to 3" wide.

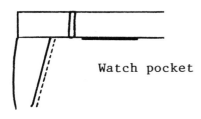

Watch pocket

1. Cut a piece of pocketing fabric 7" by the width of the pocket plus 1". Let's say your pocket will be 2½". The fabric would measure 7" x 3½".

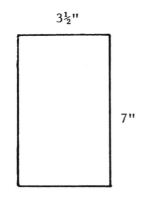

3½"

7"

2. Rip the waistband facing so it is out of the way. Rip the waist seam in the area where you'll be working too.

3. Put the pocket and the pants, right sides together, and stitch.

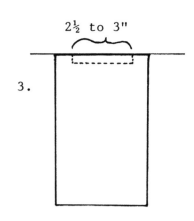

4. Slash diagonally to the corners.

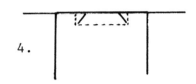

5. Turn the pocket to the wrong side of the garment and press.

6. Fold the pocket up so the edges are flush. *The pocket may gap open slightly when completed, so try to match the pocketing fabric. If you cannot get a color that blends well, take a piece of fabric from the hem and use it for facing. Sew it to the pocket so it will be behind the gap.

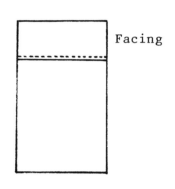

Facing

7. Sew the edges of the pocket.

8. Resew the waistband.

Waistband

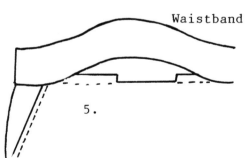

5.

8.

Outside

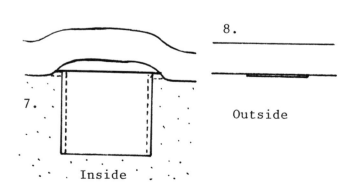

7.

Inside

116

Back Bound Pocket

It is becoming increasingly popular for ready-to-wear manufacturers to eliminate back pockets from men's pants. Because men are used to having them, you may be asked to add one or even two.

Back pockets are located about 4½" down from the top of the waistband, and are centered on the dart.

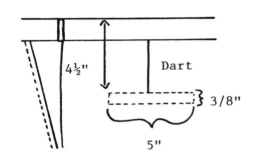

1. Sew a basting line around where the new pocket will be. Make it 5" x 3/8".

2. You will have to remove some fabric from the hems to make welts and a pocket facing. For the welts, you will need 2 strips, 1" x 6". For the facing, a piece 1" x 6" is the minimum, but 1½ or 2" x 6" would be better.

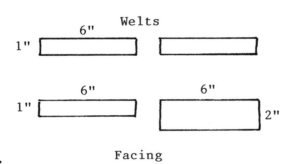

Facing

Press the welts in half lengthwise and put a basting line a little wider than 1/8" across each one.

Baste across the welt

3. Match the stitching lines of the welts up with the stitching line for the pocket and sew them in place. Do not sew the corners.

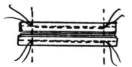

Sew welts to the pants

4. Go to the inside and slash down the middle and diagonally out to the corners.

Slash on the inside

117

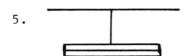

5. Turn the welts through the opening and press.

6. On the inside, sew across the little triangles, securing them to the welts.

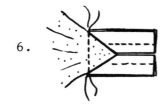

7. Cut a piece of pocketing 16" x 7".

8. Center a 7" edge on the selvage of the bottom welt and sew them, right sides together.

9. Position the facing piece on the pocket so that when the pocket is folded up, the facing will be behind the pocket opening. Sew it in place. *Note: the pocket will be folded up so that the top is flush with the waist seam, not with the top welt.

10. Fold the pocket up and stitch it to the upper welt.

11. Turn the side edges under once and under again. Stitch them down.

12. Rip the waistband facing loose and extend the top of the pocket up under it.

13. From the right side, stitch the ditch securing the waistband facing and the top of the pocket in place.

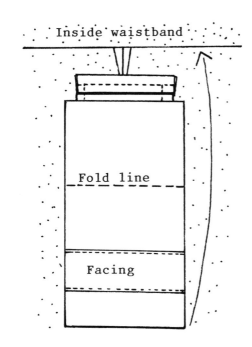

When folded up, the facing covers the welts

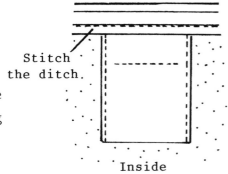

118

14. Go to the right side and bar tack the corners of the pockets. A narrow line of zig-zag will do.

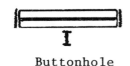

Zig-zag the corners

Buttonhole

If the customer wants a button, make a vertical buttonhole in the middle of the pocket. Sew a button to the pocket facing.

Waist Snugs

Waist snugs are sewn to the waistband facing. They are made of a rubberized material and they keep the shirt from coming untucked. Purchase them at tailoring supply stores.

1. Rip the stitching that holds the waistband facing down. You may have to remove belt loops.

Waist snugs sewn to facing

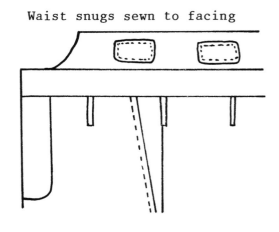

2. Space the snugs evenly around the facing and sew them on. There are usually two in the front and two in the back. The CB seam is kept free to cut down on bulk and for alteration purposes.

3. Resew the facing by stitching the ditch and resew belt loops if there were any.

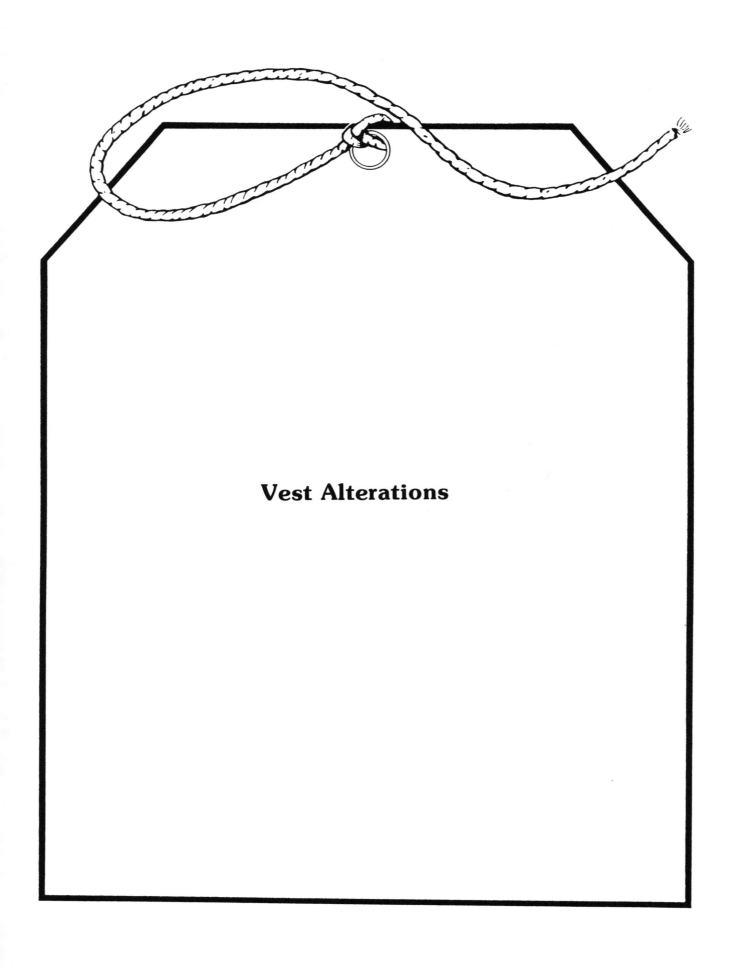

Vest Alterations

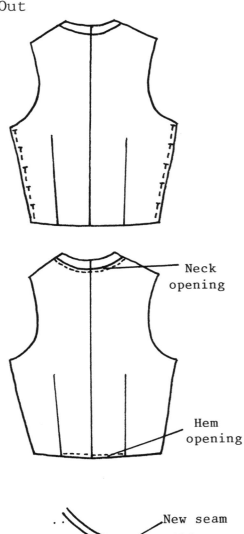

1. Pin the sideseams as needed. (If the sideseams need to be taken in past the front pocket, pin some out of the CB seam too. Take the sideseams in only up to ½" from the pocket.)

2. Open the vest at the neck where the lining is attached or at the lining bottom. If there is some topstitching part way across the CB bottom, this indicates you can open it there.

3. Pull the sideseams through the opening. The front sideseams will be encased in the back sideseams of the lining.

4. Simply sew through all thicknesses the amount needed. (Or let out as needed.)

5. Turn the vest right side out. Rip the old seam if you let out. Press and then close the opening.

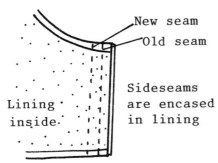

* If you need to let the vest out in excess of the sideseams, you may be able to do so by cutting a new lining. See "Making a New Back".

Center Back Seam

Open this seam to take in.

Taking In

1. Do not take in the center back seam more than 1" total or it will pull the sideseams backwards.

2. If you enter through the neck, pull the lining inside out, and sew one continuous seam right through the hem.

3. If you enter through the bottom, take in the lining and the back.

4. The center back seams are pressed to one side rather than open.

5. Turn the right side out and topstitch over the opening.

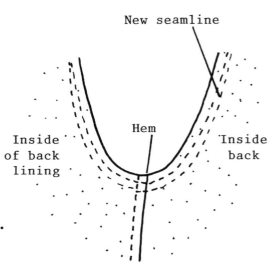

New seamline

Inside of back lining

Hem

Inside back

Letting Out

The center back seam is never let out except when absolutely necessary because the old stitching lines will usually show.

Points in Front Stick Out

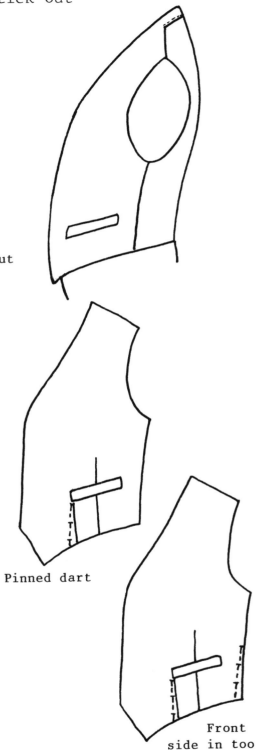

If the customer has a prom-
inent abdomen, the vest may
stick out in front at the
points.

**Points
stick out**

1. Pin a dart with the
point ending at the front
corner of the pocket.

2. If this is not enough,
pin some out of the side
front only, not the back.

Pinned dart

3. Transfer the markings
to the inside and take in.
Be sure to take in the lining
too.

**Front
side in too**

Shrinking the Lapels

This alteration is done when the lapel edges stand away from the chest.

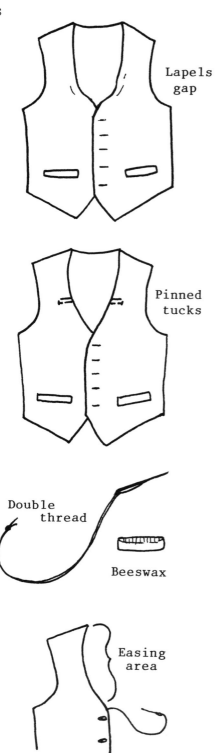

Lapels gap

1. It is hard to fit for this, and a second fitting will be required. At the first fitting, simply pin a horizontal tuck in each lapel so the fullness is removed. This tuck indicates the amount the lapels need to be shrunk. An average amount is ½". Do not guarantee results over 3/4" because amounts over that would be very difficult to shrink in.

Pinned tucks

2. Thread a needle with a double strand and tie a double knot. Wax the thread so it will be strong and tangle-free.

Double thread

Beeswax

3. You will be sewing a small running stitch along the lapel which will help you to ease out the fullness. Start at the inside bottom. Your stitches will be going in and out between the vest front and lining. They do not show.

Easing area

Gently pull the thread as you go, easing in the fullness. Steam every 2" over a ham. It's shape will
simulate the chest curve. Spongy fabric such as tweed
will respond very well. Hard finishes like gabardine
will be more difficult. Try to avoid any ripples or
gather marks. If you are easing in 3/4" or less, you
won't need to pull very hard. More than 3/4" will
require a lot of shrinking.

4. When **you** get to the top,
bring your needle out through
the ditch of the lining and
front seams.

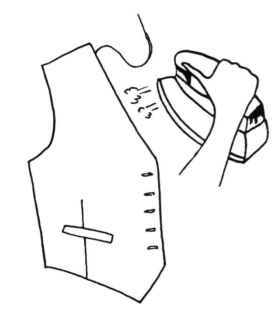

5. Put a pin in the vest
and wrap the thread around
it a few times so it is held
tightly. Secure the needle
in the vest.

6. Do the second lapel.

Thread
wrapped around
pin

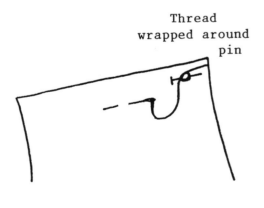

At the second fitting, you
may have to release the
thread if you have eased too
much. Remove the pin and
gently stretch the easing
out until the lapel fits.
Put the pin in and secure
the thread around it until
later when you can tie it off.

If you have not eased enough, you can try to ease in more while the customer is wearing the vest. This is not done unless the fabric has been easy to ease because you will risk breaking the thread.

If you cannot ease more in while the customer is wearing the vest, pin out a tuck as you did in the first fitting.

Pin out a tuck after you eased if there is still extra fabric.

7. When you have finally eased enough, bring the needle out on the inside of the vest. Tie a good knot and backstitch several times to secure your line of easing. Give the lapel a final press over a ham.

If you just can't ease out enough fullness, you can try taking in the shoulder seam on the front only. This may or may not help.

Take in on the front only.

Removing the Back Strap

Some men find the adjustable
back strap unnecessary or a
nuisance and will ask to have
it removed. Rip the seams
where the strap is attached
and remove it. If the customer does not want it, save
it. You may be able to use
it when another customer wants
to add a strap. Go to the
inside through the bottom or
neck and resew the sideseams.

Enter here...

or here.

Back strap

Making a New Back

Since the back of the vest is usually made of
lining fabric, it may wear out before the front does.
If it needs to be replaced, be sure to agree in advance on the fabric you will use, by asking the customer his preference.

Remove the old back and back lining. Rip out
the darts and gently press the pieces. Try not to
pull them off grain. Use the old pieces as a pattern
for the new back.

When a vest is too tight and has been let out
all possible, you may be able to replace the whole
back as above, adding the extra needed width at the
sideseams and center back.

Recutting the Neck and Shoulders

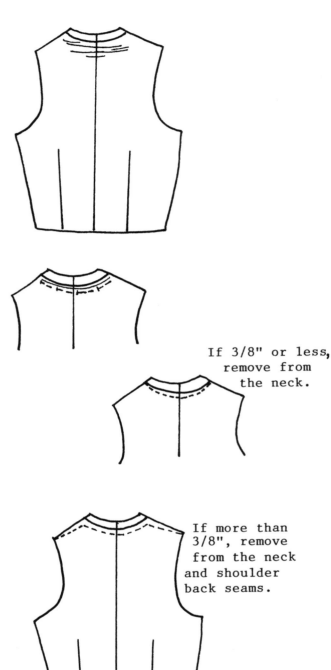

This alteration is needed when there are pull lines across the back, below the neck.

1. Pin out the fabric below the neck.

If the total amount to be removed is 3/8" or less, take it out of the neck seam.

If 3/8" or less, remove from the neck.

If the amount is more than 3/8", remove it from the neck and back shoulder seam only (not from the front).

If more than 3/8", remove from the neck and shoulder back seams.

2. Do the same alteration on the lining.

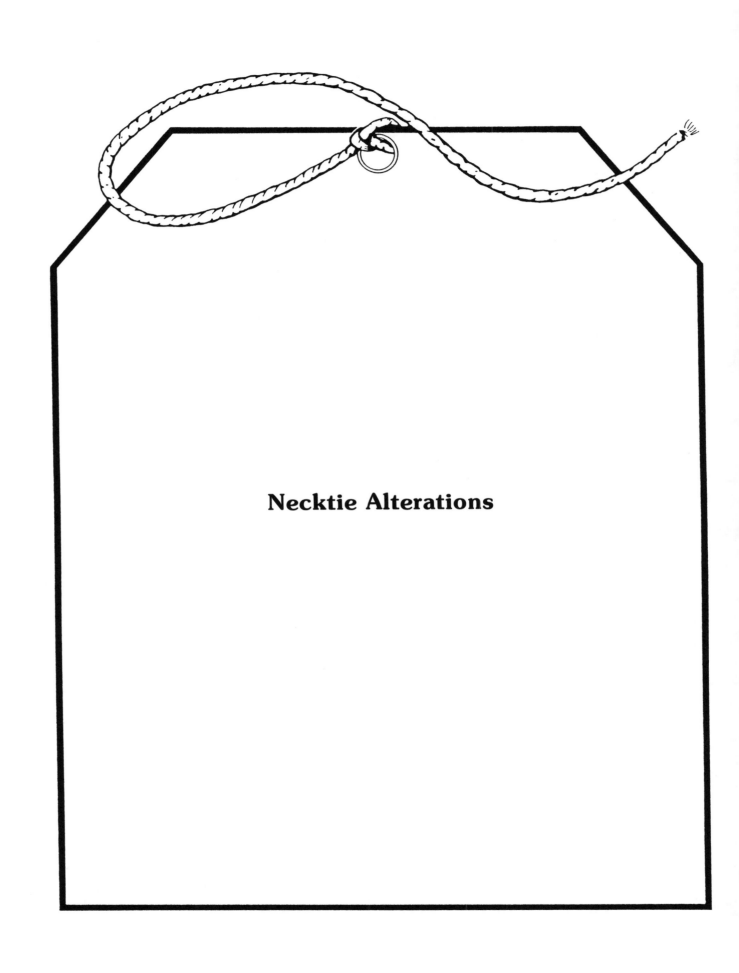

Necktie Alterations

Narrowing Neckties

Any necktie can be narrowed with excellent results in a short amount of time. However, because neckties are cut on the bias, care should be taken to keep the tie from stretching out of shape. In every step of the procedure, remember to handle the tie delicately and you will avoid the only pitfall in the process.

1. Measure the tie from point to point and figure how much width you want to remove.

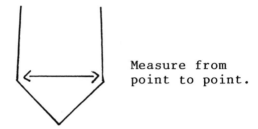

Measure from point to point.

2. Turn the tie to the back side and lay it on a flat surface, your ironing board, or pressing table. Remove the label and rip the center fold to just above the center seam of the tie. Press the tie open gently, using no back and forth movement with the iron.

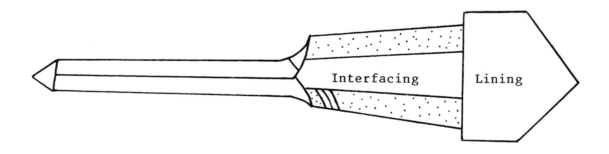

3. Take the interfacing out from beneath the lining.
Trim half the amount you are narrowing the tie off
each edge. Taper to nothing at the middle of the tie.
For instance, if you have a 4" tie and you are narrowing it to 3", you will remove a total of 1", or ½"
from each side. Then trim the same amount from the
necktie. Cut right through the edge where the lining
is attached.

Trim lines

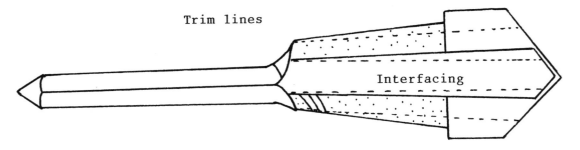

Interfacing

4. Put the interfacing back under the lining.

5. Turn one cut edge of the tie under ¼" and press.

6. Fold both edges to the middle with the folded
edge on top.

7. Holding the iron about 1" above the tie, steam the
new edges into place. Keep the tie lying flat all
the time. Measure to make sure the tie is the desired
width and the point is even. If it is not, open the
tie, steam out the area to be corrected, and steam in
a new fold.

8. Leaving the tie on a flat surface, hand stitch the
edges together, catching the interfacing but not the
front. Do not pull the stitches tight.

9. Replace the label with tiny stitches on the sides only. Some men thread the narrow end of the tie through the label so the top and bottom must be free. Sew it into place even if it was attached originally with a fusible.

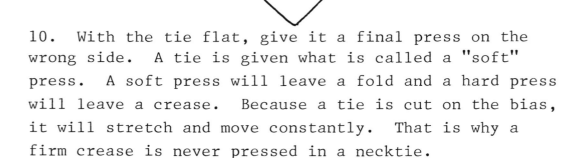

10. With the tie flat, give it a final press on the wrong side. A tie is given what is called a "soft" press. A soft press will leave a fold and a hard press will leave a crease. Because a tie is cut on the bias, it will stretch and move constantly. That is why a firm crease is never pressed in a necktie.

Hold the iron above the tie and steam it. This is a "soft" press.

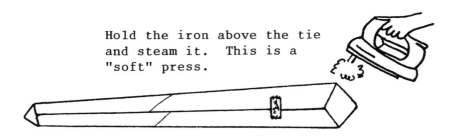

If you are narrowing more than one tie, it may be worth your while to make a cardboard pattern of the size tie you want. You can use it as a cutting guide for the interfacing and as a guide for pressing the folds, which will eliminate measuring every time.

Shortening Neckties

Ask the customer to bring in a tie that is the correct length so you can measure it. If he doesn't have one the desired length, let him knot the tie as he would wear it, and measure the excess.

1. Open the tie at the center seam.

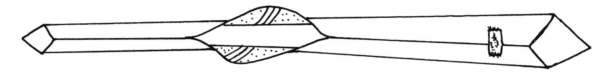

2. Cut through the interfacing diagonally and remove a piece the length the tie is to be shortened.

3. Rip the seam and cut equal amounts off each edge. For example, if the tie is to be shortened 2", cut 1" off each side. Cut diagonally, following the edges.

4. Put the edges right sides together and sew. Do not sew the interfacing into the seam.

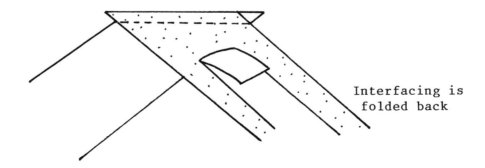

Interfacing is folded back

5.   Press the seam open.

Interfacing is folded back

6.   Fold the interfacing down on the open seam. The edges of the interfacing will be flush. Tack them to the necktie seam with a catch stitch.

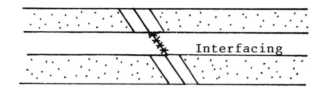

Interfacing

7.   Fold the edges of the necktie over and hand sew them together. Do not pull the stitch too tightly as you sew. Also, try not to stretch the tie.

8.   Give it a soft press on the wrong side.

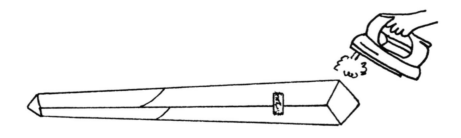

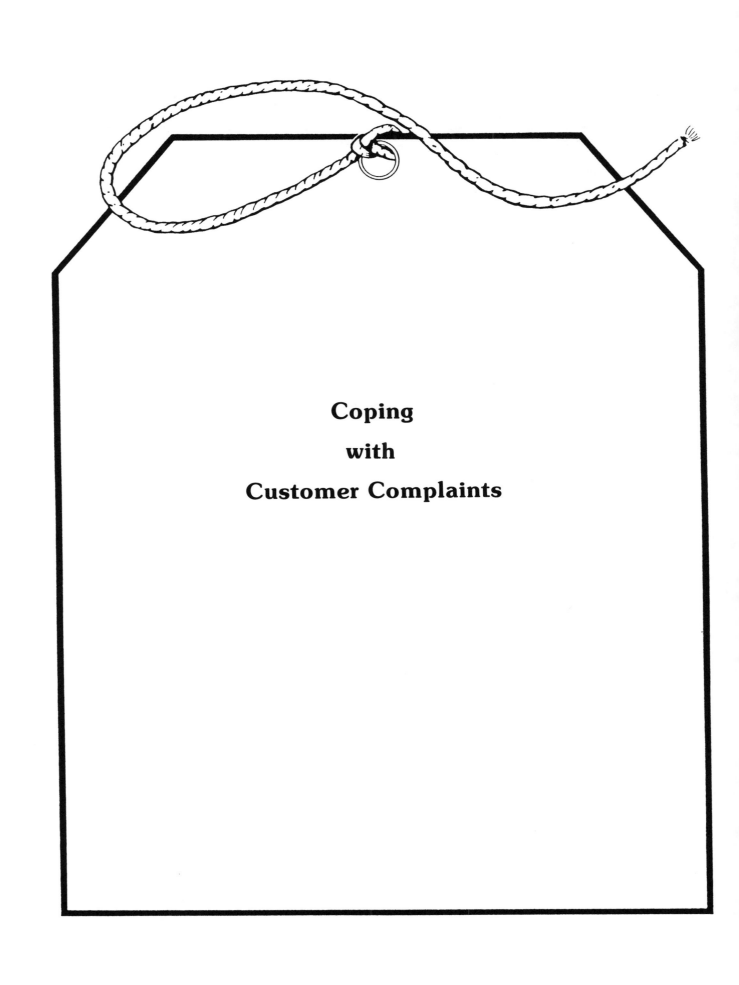

Coping

with

Customer Complaints

Men will have fewer complaints than women because they don't expect clothing to enhance their appearance as much as women do. They are less concerned with fashion, because their clothing is more regimented. They are more concerned with how the clothing feels.

No matter how reputable the business, an occasional customer complaint is unavoidable. Following are some tips that will help in this area:

* __Always do the best possible work.__ If you have fufilled your end of the bargain, there will be very few reasons for complaints.

* Make sure the customer tries the garment on when he comes to pick it up. Then you will be sure he is satisfied and he feels your work is acceptable.

* Keep accurate records of everything. You may need to refer back to them. Describe in detail the specifications for the job and write them down. Make note of and date any changes the customer may make over the phone.

* At your first meeting, specify time limits for redos and charges for them if there are any. Decide on your return policies and write them on the receipt.

* Always give receipts for everything, even for work redone or done free.

*   Be professional and businesslike with
    customers no matter how friendly you
    become with them. As a woman, it will
    be very awkward if you attempt to so-
    cialize with your male customers.

*   Never admit guilt on the phone. First
    of all, if you have done your best work,
    there will be a very slim chance that the
    complaint is legitimate. Secondly, you
    have no control over what happens to the
    garment when it leaves your place of bus-
    iness, so reserve comment until you see
    it. Say you are sorry there is a problem
    and ask when would be a convenient time
    to get together.

*   Always remain calm, even if the customer
    is not. If the complaint turns out to be
    a legitimate one, fix it cheerfully. Ex-
    amples of illegitimate complaints would be
    wanting a hem change after not bringing the
    proper shoes to the fitting, and wanting
    free alterations after gaining or losing
    weight. If the customer is wrong, try not
    to be accusing or sarcastic. By referring
    to the receipt, you should be able to find
    who is in error without pointing a finger.
    Most problems arise out of misunderstand-
    ings and can be solved without ill feelings.

In general, when dealing with customers, present
yourself as a professional. They will return if they
are satisfied with your efficiency.

Suggested Price List

The following price list has been compiled over the last fifteen years from price lists nationwide, and from my own experience. It is meant to be used as a guide and should be adjusted according to your location, your skill level, and your experience. You should revise your prices at least once a year. The best price list is one that you feel comfortable with and that is profitable for you. There will always be jobs that will be difficult to quote a set price for. I recommend you charge by the hour for those.

Coats (Suit or Overcoat)

```
Sleeves- shorten or lengthen ................. $8.00-17.50
         with vents ........................... add 5.00
         lengthen and face ................... add 10.00
         raincoat, moving tabs .............. add 4.00
         narrowing ........................... 17.50
         correcting sleeve pitch ............. 27.50-35.00
Sideseams- in or out with CB vent ............ 17.50
         with double vents .............. add 6.00
         lined ......................... add 5.00
         into armholes, unlined ............ 25.00
            lined ............................ add 7.50
         CB seam in or out ...................10.00
            lined ............................ add 5.00
Darts- in or out ............................. 12.00
Shoulders- narrowing .......................... 35.00-45.00
         dropping ........................... 37.50-50.00
Shortening- unlined ........................... 22.5
         lined ............................... 35.00-40.00
         raincoat ........................... 25.00-35.00
         leather ............................ 30.00-50.00
Collars- lowering ...........................17.50
         and squaring  shoulders ............. add 10.00
         shortening .......................... 35.00-45.00
Lapels- shrinking .............................15.00
         narrowing ........................... 35.00-50.00
Vents- close .................................12.50
         add .......................................17.50
```

```
Interlining- partial ......................... 35.00
              total body ..................... 65.00
              (prices do not include fabric)
Relining- not including fabric .............. 75.00
Shoulder pads- add, each ......................7.50
Buttons- resew, each ..........................2.00
Buttonholes- hand work .......................10.00
Zippers- replace jacket front ............... 17.50
         ski jacket pocket ...................12.00
         (prices do not include zippers)
```

Shirts

```
Sleeves- shorten .............................12.50
         move vent ....................... add 5.00
         make short sleeves ..................10.00
Shorten- .....................................12.00
Darts- add, ...................................8.00
Sideseams- plain .............................10.00
           flat felled ...................... 20.00
Collars- narrowing ...........................12.00
         add buttons and buttonholes ..........7.50
Emblems- add ..................................5.00
```

Pants

```
Hems- plain bottom, shorten or lengthen.    8.00-15.00
      cuffs .............................    add 5.00
      lengthen and face .................    add 7.50
      heel guards .......................add 4.00
      levis .............................10.00-15.00
      with zippers ......................add 10.00
Waist and seat- in or out ......................10.00-15.00
               seat only .....................7.50-10.00
Waist, seat, stride- in or out .............. 17.50
                    stride only .............12.50
Crotch- in or out .............................10.00
        add crotchpiece .......................15.00
        reshape ...............................7.50
        lining ...............................12.50
Sideseams- in or out ......................... 15.00
           redo pockets ...................... 27.50
Dropping the waistband- ...................... 27.50-40.00
                move watch pocket, add ..12.50
                move fly facing ..... add 7.50
Tapering pant legs- .......................... 17.50-25.00
Swing creases- each leg ......................12.50
Line- to knees ............................... 17.50
      complete ............................... 35.00-45.00
      (prices do not include fabric)
```

Replace zipper- 15.00
          (Price does not include zipper)
Belt loops- add 10.00
            make new 17.50
Waist snugs- 10.00
Pockets- new half pocket 10.00
         new whole pocket 17.50
         new watch pocket 10.00
         new back bound pocket 17.50

Vests

Sideseams- in or out 15.00
           front or back only 25.00
Center Back seam- 12.50
Points stick out- 10.00
Shrink lapels- 12.50
Removing back strap- 7.50
Make a new back- fabric not included 30.00
Recut neck and shoulders 17.50-25.00

Neckties

Narrowing- 10.00-15.00
Shortening- 10.00

Index

Other Publications by Mary Roehr

Sewing As A Home Business tells how to start and operate a sewing business in your home. It includes licensing, taxes, advertising, customer relations, target markets, bookkeeping, financing, and insurance and more. There are complete price lists for custom sewing and alterations for men and women which are good nationwide, and discussion on how to figure an hourly rate. Learn how to price a product or craft. If you have a sewing business in your home or have thought about starting one, this book is for you! $14.95

Altering Men's Ready-to-Wear is 150 pages with hundreds of illustrations. Pictures show how to identify the problem and what to do to correct it. Included are pants, shirts, jackets, coats, vests, and neckties. Marking, pressing, hand sewing, and prices for men's alterations are there too. A handy index will help you locate the solution to your problem quickly. If you have wanted to alter men's clothing, now is the time to start! $17.95

Speed Tailoring is a completely illustrated spiral-bound book that explains the fastest and easiest way to construct a woman's lined jacket or coat using all the new speed techniques. It includes instructions on the use of fusible interfacing, machine shoulder pad application, professional collar and lapel placement (as done in ready-to-wear), cutting, marking, finishing, pressing methods, and more. Drawings are clear and directions are easy to follow. $14.95

Pressing to Perfection is the 1-hour companion video to *Speed Tailoring*. Author and tailor, Mary Roehr demonstrates the principles of pressing and the use of fusible interfacing so even beginning seamstresses can succeed in tailoring projects. She discusses pressing equipment, chestpiece and twill tape application, the difference between a hard press and a soft press, how to look taller and thinner by pressing, and much more. See how tailors actually do the final press on a jacket or coat. $24.95

Sew Hilarious is sewing's first cartoon book. Laugh to 64 pages of hilarious cartoons that pertain to all aspects of sewing including learning to sew, sewing equipment and materials, sewing as therapy, sewing getaways, sewing for others, and more. Anyone who sews will see themselves in the last chapter, "The Life of a Fabriholic." This book makes a great gift! $9.95

Mary Roehr Books & Video
500 Saddlerock Circle, Sedona, AZ 86336
520-282-4971

Please add $2.50 postage for first item, $1 each additional.
Check, Money Order, Visa, Mastercard, Discover, Novus, American Express